MY WORST HIRE &
WHAT I LEARNED
FROM IT

WHAT OTHERS ARE SAYING ABOUT
MY WORST HIRE & WHAT I LEARNED
FROM IT

"This is a fun and engaging quick read of the many things that can go wrong when hiring talent, and makes clear the substantial costs in dollars, morale and company culture when a "wrong hire" is made."

PROFESSOR RICK HACKETT, Professor and Canada Research Chair at McMaster University

"Craig has really provided a very practical, example based, prescriptive guide to what to do and, more important, what not to do around critical hires. In reading the book I found myself reliving some of the hiring mistakes Craig has highlighted. A great guide and a great reminder around the importance of not only job specific skills but cultural fit given the impact the hire will have on the company overall".

JEFF RUSHTON, President and CEO – Media Resources

"After reading *My Worst Hire & What I Learned From It*, Groucho Marx famous line came to mind, 'Learn from the mistakes of others as you'll never have time to make them all yourself!'"

JENNIFER FOSTER, Senior Vice President, Human Resources & Corporate Affairs at Western Forest Products

"Hiring is a crucial topic for all the leaders today. The business losses are more than time, money, and effort by recruiting, hiring, and training people who perhaps shouldn't have been brought on in the first place. Bad hiring can also impact a lot on the culture and branding of an organization, apart from the candidate experience, employee morale, and motivation. Craig's book is a great opportunity and asset for all the leaders, recruiters, HRs, and hiring managers to learn from his diversified experiences in hiring."

SOUMYASANTO (SOUMYA) SEN, Founder I Digital & Work Revolution Strategist, People Conscience

"Too many of these stories ring true from my own experiences to allow me to cast judgment on any. If there are two principles I would point to as being most critical, they are these: trust your gut, and don't ever fall in love with your own decisions. Take time. Don't rush. Never settle. This book proves these principles time and time again."

ALAN DICK – Principal at Impactful.ly

978-1-7773645-3-3 (Hardcover)
978-1-7773645-1-9 (eBook)
978-1-7773645-0-2 (Paperback)
978-1-7773645-2-6 (Audiobook)

Cover design by Fiaz Irfan
Interior design by Dania Zafar
Editing by Alex Steiner

MY WORST HIRE & WHAT I LEARNED FROM IT

CRAIG BISSETT

Hiring teams need to remember that the results of a hiring decision have the potential to positively or negatively impact so many lives. When you get the hire right the new employee's life is enhanced and teams thrive with the addition of a new valuable asset. Get the hire wrong and the quality of these same lives are adversely impacted and the team culture and bottom line of the organization are put at risk!

By
Craig Bissett

Dedicated to Kathy, the love of my life and to the growing GKJB clan.

CONTENTS

Preface

FINDING YOUR NUGGET

When I was young, our family went on vacation to an old mining town that had been replicated to look exactly like it might have during the time of the gold rush in the 1800's. In those gold rush days, people from all over North America traveled to these little towns to seek their fortune mining for gold.

The main road was lined with replicated old buildings such as the town saloon, the general store, the blacksmith, and each individual proprietor was dressed appropriately for that era. The main street was a dusty old dirt road with real stagecoaches and men on horses riding up and down right in front of the visitors.

One of the highlights of the little town was a building at the end of the main street where the gold prospectors would bring their newly discovered nuggets of gold for weighing and payment. When entering the building as a tourist, you were greeted by an old gold prospector who handed you a gold pan and directed you to the stream at the back of the property to try your hand at panning for gold. It really was a great experience, but what we discovered very quickly was that panning for gold was no easy task and a lot of hard work. That is until the old gold prospector came back to the stream where we were panning and instructed us on some practical tips. These included how to hold the pan, how to use the water in the stream to sift out the sand and rocks from the pan, and most importantly how to distinguish between what was fools gold and what was a true gold nugget.

Hiring is a little like panning for gold. At first, interviewing and assessing a candidate may seem easy, but once you start spending time with candidates you quickly realize hiring is not as easy as it first appeared to be. The contributors in this book are like the old, wise prospector who taught us how to pan for gold. Through costly hiring mistakes, these contributors have learned the hard way to get their hiring right and are willing to share their stories and lessons with you. The learning nuggets provided in this book are worth their weight in gold when hiring for today's or future roles.

MY WORST HIRE

Welcome to *My Worst Hire & What I Learned From It!*

The genesis of this book started almost immediately after we began our Hire Results Ltd business back in 2002. The premise of our business is that there is little relationship between how a candidate interviews and how they engage and perform on the job. Only once a newly hired candidate begins performing key elements of the role will the hiring team really know who they have hired. Our client base is made up of industry leaders, and it was not uncommon for a client to pull one of our consultants aside and tell them about a very costly hiring mistake they had made in the past. These remarkable stories are all about where the hire went wrong, the cost of the mistake, and most importantly what the client learned from the mistake. In each of these stories there was a lesson the client wanted to share.

After hearing story after story of hiring mistakes and these valuable learning nuggets, I wondered if hiring managers might benefit from the wisdom of other business professionals in a tangible format. It didn't take long to find our contributors for the book. A common thread between each contributor was their true desire to give back, and hopefully help the reader learn from their mistakes to make profitable and team building hiring decisions in the future.

Each story in this book has a cost associated to the mistake. As a rough estimate, these "worst hire" stories represent hard and soft costs in the range of $24,000,000. This is an average of just under $500,000.00 per hiring mistake. Just one learning nugget from the book applied to a future hiring situation could be worth $500,000 to your organization.

The Prosperity Only Candidate

JIM LAWSON

Over Jim's career he has chaired or co-chaired a multitude of recruitment committees ranging from a top tier legal firm to a multinational steel producer. He is no stranger to hiring all levels of talent, from entry level lawyers to CEO's reporting into him while in the Chairman capacity. One of Jim's hiring mantras is that a proven, successful leader can successfully manage in any industry, and that hiring teams should never get caught up in looking for industry experience alone. He believes you can take a great professional football coach and they will be equally successful coaching a team in a completely different sport. It is all about leadership!

It is within this understanding of Jim's hiring mantra where Jim made one of the worst hiring mistakes of his career. At the time, Jim was Chairman and the company required a new CEO who had the capability to lead them out of an exceedingly difficult time in the history of the company. The board insisted and pushed the leadership team and search firm to recruit and hire a candidate who was well known and respected in the industry. The search was kicked off but only candidates who knew their business and industry were shortlisted. After a long drawn out search a successful candidate was hired in the role of CEO.

Within months the board was getting signs from the leadership team that potentially a mistake had taken place in the selection of the CEO. The issue was clear, the new CEO had all the right industry experience but had only managed upward moving, successful organizations. This person had never had to manage a firm that was struggling— specifically in the area that Jim's company was struggling. This CEO simply was unable to relate or deal with the ongoing issues and did not have the capability to lead in the current environment. After much anguish Jim had to release the new CEO.

COST

Jim believes the company forfeited $2 million in cost and value to the organization because of the poor hiring decision.

JIM LAWSON

Jim is CEO of Woodbine Entertainment Group, Canada's largest racetrack operator, past Chairman of the Canadian Football League and also served twice as the interim Commissioner of the CFL. Mr. Lawson was a partner at Torys LLP and at Davies Ward Phillips & Vineberg LLP and has served on a number of private and public boards. Mr. Lawson is a graduate of Brown University (A.B.) and University of Western Ontario (LLB).

Don't think your team can solve the problems of a struggling company with a new leader who has only managed during times of growth and prosperity. Dig deep to understand how each candidate will lead in your current reality. A proven turnaround leader from outside your industry should be on your shortlist of candidates.

Blinded By Competence

DON SIMMONDS

O ver Don's career as a business leader and entrepreneur he estimates that he has been involved in over 1000 direct hires at all levels of the organization.

Don's story revolves around a divisional VP who was leading the strategic growth of one of the divisions in his company. Don's philosophy in these senior roles is always to empower the leader to lead and then get out of the way.

As a highly structured and process driven company, it was expected that each leader would lead by example, following the well-defined processes put in place for all employees. The interview and assessment process for all senior candidates was centered around the competencies of character, collaboration, and competence. As Don remembers this worst hire experience, he can pinpoint exactly where it went wrong. In the interview process and other due-diligence tasks for assessing the candidate, Don and the team covered and confirmed all the key competencies required for the role but failed to counter balance these competencies with regards to the candidate's internal motives.

The hire was completed and within six months the team

was falling apart due to the fact that the new VP's motives were entirely self-directed towards what was best for him alone. The management style of this new hire completely missed the mark concerning team collaboration and working for the good of everyone involved.

To add to the hiring mistake, the VP demanded that all his staff strictly follow the company policies and procedures while he blatantly ignored them. The team lost complete confidence and trust in the VP and ultimately, severing the business relationship was painful, lengthy, and very costly in all aspects of the business.

COST:

Lost team members, lost opportunity in the business and stress on senior management. Could be in the millions.

DON SIMMONDS

Don is Chairman and CEO, Blyth Group. Don is an executive leader and "serial entrepreneur" having founded and/or led more than 30 start-ups. Blyth Group is a Family Office and Incubator. The Simmonds family started Clearnet, one of Canada's 3 wireless networks sold to Telus in 2001 and in 1997 Don founded AirIQ, one of the first Canadian companies to combine GPS and wireless technologies. Don is the Chancellor of Crandall University in Moncton, NB and a Director of Baylin.

The more competent the candidate, the harder you must force yourself to uncover what drives their personal and business motives. A highly competent candidate can blind you in your assessment process. Park your emotions at the door and use every possible tool and method to discover their motives.

Letting Your Star Go

MATTHEW REGAN

Matt skipped university and went right into Real Estate and now runs The Regan Team, which has evolved into one of the nations top performers.

Matt was growing his real estate business and to meet his growth plans he needed to hire some aggressive and driven sales professionals. Matt put the word out on the street that he was hiring and started to receive applications. To his surprise he received a resume from someone he knew from the past. From what he knew of this particular candidate, she had some real potential to be a good salesperson but he also remembered that she was also known to have a disruptive attitude.

Bypassing his concern over the "bad behavior" attributes, Matt weighed more heavily on the candidate's potential to be a solid salesperson and hired her. This new hire turned out to be one of Matt's top producers in a short period of time. On the downside though, no one wanted to work with this person. As Matt said, "she was hitting her numbers out of the park, but everyone tried to avoid her at the office."

Matt was in a real dilemma. "Do I put up with the

disruptive behavior and reap the sales rewards or do I let the top performer go and risk lost revenue?" Matt mulled over this decision for at least a year but during this time the office environment grew tenfold in its toxicity. Matt finally decided to terminate the salesperson which resulted in a less tense and more productive work environment. Matt's concern of losing sales revenue proved to be wrong. The bonus was that sales grew rather than diminished after the disruptive salesperson left.

COST:

Rough estimate between $750,000 to $1,000,000 due to impact on other personnel within the company.

MATTHEW REGAN

Matthew is President of The Regan Team. Matt skipped university and went right into Real Estate and now runs The Regan Team, an award winning firm that has evolved into one of the nation's top performers.

Do not let fear of financial loss influence your decision-making once you realize you have made a costly hiring mistake. The longer a leader waits to terminate a bad hire (even if they are a star salesperson), the bigger the negative impact will be to the company.

The Cost of Hiring #2

CHRIS BARRETT

C hris is a born entrepreneur. From owning multiple pub restaurants to running one of the fastest growing online marketing companies, he has had his share of costly bad hires.

Chris's worst hire happened amid acquiring a major competitor. Once the merger had taken place, Chris found himself having to evaluate two internal candidates for a newly created senior manager role. After a few in-depth interviews with both candidates, a decision was made to offer the job to the candidate who had proven himself in his past role while working with Chris. He was clearly the #1 choice. However, much to Chris' surprise, before the offer was even made, this same candidate submitted his resignation, and the team was not able to convince him to stay. Immediately a decision was made to make the #2 candidate the offer. Chris needed to get this manager in the newly created role ASAP and they believed they had a "good enough" candidate. As Chris remembers, the team viewed the #2 candidate as possessing 80% of the 1st candidate's abilities and potential. In a pinch and under pressure however, they determined that 80% was better than not having any candidates so the offer was made and accepted.

Within six months, Chris realized that the hired manager was not only 20% less than his #1 choice, but also that the 18-person team was starting to run at the same level as the manager. The mistake was now being multiplied throughout the team and the impact was significant. Chris hoped it would correct itself but after two years he had to terminate the senior manager.

COST:

The true cost would be close to $2 million over the two years.

CHRIS BARRETT

Chris is CEO of Operatic Agency, a creative digital agency that solves business challenges with data-driven strategies. Chris holds a Master's Degree focused on organizational design and behavioural psychology and undergraduate degrees in Marketing and Economics.

Never compromise when hiring management. If your #1 candidate turns down your offer—resist the temptation to hire the #2 candidate. Go back and search for the next #1 candidate. The cost of hiring #2, if wrong, will be multiplied throughout the team.

The Value of Your Value Statement

BILL GEORGE

Bill is a best-selling author and has served in the U.S. Department of Defense. He has taught Leadership in his role as Professor of Management Practices at Harvard Business School and has served as Chairman and CEO at Medtronic, along with Senior Executive roles with Honeywell and Litton Industries.

Bill was the CEO of a company that was growing 18% annually back during the dotcom days. He and his team were in desperate need of a highly qualified CIO to be part of the executive team and lead the technology division.

The values of the company were very clear: "Restore people to full life and health." Their mission and the purpose of the company was all about the restoration of health for their clients. For this reason, it was critical that the executive team was on the same page concerning these clearly stated values. Part of the company philosophy was to treat all employees equally. The executive team was compensated well but there were no real extra perks for those in senior management.

The new CIO had been interviewed multiple times and was clearly the most qualified technical individual for the job. Bill thought the team philosophy had been clearly explained to the new hire—specifically the fact that perks were not part of the management philosophy. However, Bill saw the first of many cracks in the armor of the new hire during their first offsite meeting as an executive team. The new CIO approached the head of HR requesting some very unusual perks, knowing that the company had a strict "No Perk" policy. It was not one request but many. Within the first 4 days on the job Bill knew he had a major mistake on his hands. Bill and the team had checked out everything except the candidate's values!

COST:

$200,000 plus lost credibility within the team.

BILL GEORGE

Bill George is Senior Fellow at Harvard Business School, where he has taught leadership since 2004, the author of Discover Your True North, and former Chair & CEO of Medtronic. He has served on the board of Directors of Goldman Sachs, ExxonMobil, Novartis, Target and Mayo Clinic.

If you have a company mission and value statement, don't leave it hanging on the wall. Take it into the interview process and assess the candidate based on what the company believes and wants in a culture. The candidate may have all the right skills, but if they don't fit your company values, you have a major mistake on your hands.

Is the Search Firm's Short List Really Your Shortlist?

NANCY MACKAY

Nancy's story has a great angle that has not been covered in our interviews and one that needs to be heard by anyone using recruitment firms to source candidates.

Due diligence is key to managing risk in any investment. It's easy for a supplier of services to your company to tell you what you want to hear but key to a good outcome is ensuring that they know what you want from them. In Nancy's case, a recruitment firm was recommended to her by a close business associate as Nancy's company was ready to begin searching for a new senior business development professional. Rather than investigating and meeting multiple firms to fully understand their value propositions, Nancy hired the firm referred to her. At the time, Nancy's company relied heavily on net new business being won by a small sales team that were "outcome" focused.

Looking back, Nancy recalls that the meeting with the recruitment firm focused solely on the experience and skills the candidates required for the role. There was no discussion concerning culture fit or the overall values and mindset of the company. The shortlist of candidates presented by the recruitment firm all had great experience but none of them were screened for culture fit. The candidate that was ultimately hired had excelled during the interview process due to the skills-based questions provided by the recruitment firm. The hiring decision was made with no consideration of "outcome mindset" and "results oriented" sales culture. The results: within 60 days the candidate was let go due to a complete misalignment with the mindset of the company.

Nancy was set up for failure from the first meeting with the recruitment firm. They were looking simply for skills and not attributes.

COST:

The cost of the mistake was in the $100,000 range.

NANCY MACKAY

Dr. Nancy MacKay is the CEO & Founder of MacKay CEO Forums. MCF has 1200+ members around the world involved with over 100 peer learning groups and 60+ Forum Chairs who are very successful trusted advisors. Nancy is a coach to CEOs, executives, business owners and trusted advisors around the world, a dynamic keynote speaker and published author.

When deciding to use a recruitment firm, invest the time by inviting multiple firms to compete for the business. Listen to where they focus the conversation. Is it solely based on tactical skills, or is the conversation also directed towards team and culture fit? Ensure you understand not only how candidates will be recruited but also how they will be assessed before being presented in a short list.

A Detective Mindset for the Hidden Clue

JOHN SLEEMAN

O ver John's business career he has invested and started four businesses and he would say much of the success he has achieved has been through the people that have joined his companies in senior leadership roles. One of the attributes John looks for in a leader is a well-balanced make-up of confidence and humility; confidence in their abilities and talent but not having a swollen head about it. It is in this personality make-up where John found himself making a significant hiring mistake.

While hiring for a senior executive in the company, John used his standard hiring process which entailed instinct (gained over the years) plus multiple touch points with the candidates in different settings to get a feel for their fit with his team. This particular hire came with all the trimmings of a very strong resume and was very impressive in the interview. However, John did notice throughout the hiring process the candidate's ability to always turn the conversation around to himself. John noted this "self-serving" personality but decided to dismiss it and cut the candidate some slack. The candidate's impressive resume made up for this concern so the hire was made.

Alarm bells went off 2 weeks into the hire when John arrived at the office just as new, high-end office furniture was being delivered for his new executive. John admits to having given the go ahead for an office spruce up but was somewhat taken aback when that spruce up involved furniture and fittings that were superior to those in other executive offices. Maybe John's instincts at the start of the hiring process regarding this individual's personality were right. For the next 6 months until the executive was dismissed, an attitude of entitlement and arrogance was being noticed by key staff and board members and the question swirling was, "When was John going to deal with this misaligned executive's attitude?" Once the executive was let go, many in the office expressed their appreciation to John for finally taking action.

COST:

North of $100,000.

JOHN SLEEMAN

John Sleeman is Founder and Chair of Sleeman Breweries Ltd. At 23 he launched his first business, a pub, followed by The Imported Beer Company. In 1985, he restarted his family's Sleeman Brewing and Malting Company. In 2019 he opened Spring Mill Distillery, located in Guelph, Ontario. Mr. Sleeman's career has included many Boards and Organizations. He has received an honourary degree from the University of Guelph and is a recipient of the Order of Canada.

Given enough time together, candidates will drop hints to assist you in getting a glimpse of their true self. It is your job to listen for these clues. The combination of clues and instinct can be a powerful equation for seeing through a padded resume and honed interview skills.

Rolling Up Your Sleeves

JAY STEINFELD

J ay is founder and CEO of Blinds.com—one of the world's largest online window covering stores.

To this day Jay will take as much time as he needs before hiring a single individual due in part to the costly mistakes he made when his company was just getting off the ground. Jay's worst hire took place as his small company was expanding and he needed to hire the most important role in the company: a director of online marketing. Due to the e-commerce nature of his company, online marketing was one of the most important roles for future growth.

The candidate in question came from a large reputable organization and had been highly recommended to Jay by a business associate. In the interview Jay was impressed with the candidate's industry knowledge but Jay's downfall was his failure to explain the "hands-on" requirements of the job. Jay assumed the candidate was used to getting his hands into the day to day tactical marketing elements of the job. At the time, the company didn't have any structured hiring process or defined job description.

The position of director of online marketing was offered

and accepted, without further ado. What Jay quickly discovered, once the new hire started, was that his new online director excelled in managing people but had not been hands on in any sort of tactical marketing functions for years. He had little ability or confidence performing some of the most basic online marketing tasks. As Jay remembers, "I assumed the newly hired employee understood that they would have to be hands on and roll up their sleeves. The problem was the candidate was very good at talking about online marketing, directing people to do the online tasks but was not able to do the tasks himself. The hire was a disaster and the cost to the company was significant in lost market share. We had to let the new hire go and start the search again."

COST:

Critical market share.

JAY STEINFELD

Jay is the Founder and CEO of Global Custom Commerce (Blinds.com) (GCC), the world's #1 online window coverings store. In January 2014, GCC merged with The Home Depot, when he continued to lead the company as its CEO and joined the Home Depot Online Leadership Team. GCC has been recognized multiple times as The Best Place to Work in Houston, Top 5 Workplaces in Texas, one of the 50 Most Engaged Workplaces in America, the American Marketing Association Marketer of the Year, and many others. Jay is an Ernst and Young Entrepreneur of the Year and has earned a Lifetime Achievement Award by the Houston Technology Center.

Be extremely careful when hiring
someone who is from a different
sized operation. If you are a small
company and the candidate is
coming from a large, well-financed
firm, make sure they will roll up
their sleeves and do the grunt work
required for your growth plans.
Ensure new hires know what they are
getting into.

The Internal Promotion

SAM REESE

Sam has been the CEO of one of the largest global sales performance companies and has also run sales teams with Kinkos and British Telecom.

While in the role of vice president of sales of a large commercial sales division, Sam found himself needing to create a new role between himself and the regional sales managers. Sam's choice was an internal sales manager, but this meant that now he would have to back fill the sales manager's role. This now open sales manager's role happened to be in the most strategic and critical region in the company. This was one division where a bad hire would be disastrous and extremely costly.

The search for the new sales manager began with both external and internal candidates but in Sam's mind he had already chosen who he wanted in the role. The candidate was from inside the company and had been a top sales performer. When Sam interviewed the candidate he heavily relied on past sales performance and let his guard down during the interview. As Sam remembers, the interview was more of a casual meeting. Sam made no concerted effort to try to understand the candidate's ability to lead a team. Sam admits that there were many warning signs; comments from internal team members and things he saw in the casual interview with the candidate. In retrospect, Sam admits that he only wanted to hear what he wanted to hear and turned a blind eye to all the warning signs. The new sales manager was hired.

The damage was done, and the region struggled terribly. The new sales manager wanted to sell but did not want to manage and the whole team suffered. Sam had to demote the newly promoted manager, and within six months he left and joined a competitor.

COST:

From lost accounts, unproductive regional sales, and disruption to team—minimum $500,000.

SAM REESE

Sam spent his early career in sales and leadership positions in Xerox and British Telecom, and has been a CEO for over 20 years. As the CEO of Vistage Worldwide for the past 4 years, Sam leads the world's largest CEO membership advisory firm. He is the author of two published books on global account management, an experienced keynote speaker and was a former All-American track athlete.

The requirements of a sales manager are completely different from a high producing salesperson. Don't let your guard down, especially if the candidate is an internal salesperson. Force yourself to dig deep, make sure you view the internal candidate in the interview process as if you didn't know their past.

The Real Motive Why They Want the Job

ESTHER DE WOLDE

E sther's retractable screen door business is built around
blending indoor and outdoor living together. She wishes
she had given intuition its fair due as a significant part
of a strong hiring process that would have prevented her from
making her worst hiring mistake a few years ago.

Esther needed to hire a 2IC (2nd In Command) for a key
role within her manufacturing facility. There had been some
costly hiring mistakes in this department in the past, and now
Esther wanted to bring in a more experienced professional
who could successfully liaison between all the different
departments and be content in the role.

Esther has a methodical approach to hiring and believes
in having multiple touch points with a candidate before any
hire is made. Having done her due diligence, the short list
of candidates pointed to one candidate in particular whose
previous positions were more senior roles. Throughout the
multiple interviews and touch points, Esther approached
the subject of how content the candidate would be in a 2IC

position. The candidate made a compelling case as to why they would not have a problem being second in command, but something didn't sit right with Esther. After fighting her internal concerns of over hiring for the role, Esther gave in and made the offer. Shortly after the probation period was up, signs of undermining the new hire's boss started to appear, and before long it was clear this person had only one goal—get the top job in the department at any cost. Esther unsuccessfully attempted to coach this new hire, but it was hopeless: the new 2IC was power hungry. Esther had the unpleasant and costly task of terminating the employee after much internal disruption. Esther could not resist validating the earlier affirmation shared by the employee to which they said "Yes, I did say that. But I didn't say second to which position". Clearly a case of a specifically-chosen reply in the original interview that Esther did not pick up on.

COST:

Recruiting and Training Project gone bust because of their arrogance, including damaged trust with our customers and vendor—$250,000.

ESTHER DE WOLDE

Esther is the CEO and Co-Founder of Phantom Screens. As a CGA/CPA, she has nurtured and grown the corporation to become the leading brand in the retractable screen industry. Esther is a member of several local and global boards and a Youth Leader in her church. Being a country farm girl at heart, she loves nothing more than spending time working in her English garden. With their 2 daughters grown, she also loves golfing with her husband.

It is extremely hard for most candidates to take a salary or promotion cut and remain content. Be careful when a candidate applies for a role that is below their current/ past position or compensation. They may have what you want but make sure you do your best to understand their real motives for taking the role.

Don't Be Afraid to Change Up the Team

JOHN MCLENNAN

John has run both entrepreneurial and large organizations in North America and understands the need to have the right executive team in place to achieve the company's goals. John's view on running a business works on a 36-month planning cycle with a leadership team that is customized for the expected results based on a clear vision of what the organization must achieve for success.

John's worst hire started off as one of his best hires. The company John was leading was going through significant change at all levels of the business due to aggressive new competition. The company required a shakeup to be forcefully steered in a direction many of the employees did not want to go, but it had to be done to survive. John needed to hire a senior executive that was not afraid to ruffle feathers and lead in a manner that was borderline aggressively disruptive. The hire was exactly what the company needed to forge ahead, and after a tumultuous two years, the turnaround was well under way. The company was moving in the right direction.

At this point, the senior executive was asked by John multiple times to ease up on the aggressive behavior, but it didn't take too long for John to recognize that this executive's internal nature only had one mode: intense aggression. The great hire of two years prior was now being asked to change direction, to perform in a different way, but he quickly became John's worst hire and a significant detriment to the company. It took too long to move the "good to worst" hire out of the company which resulted in significant morale issues.

COST:

Employee morale was negatively affected due to overly aggressive leadership.

JOHN MCLENNAN

John has an impressive history of leading world brands from being CEO of BCE Mobile, Bell Canada, AT & T Canada/Allstream and Cantel. He has been Executive Vice President of Mitel Corporation and Corporate Director at various Public and Private Corporations. John is a graduate of Clarkson University Potsdam, New York with his BSC and MSc.

When hiring for executive team members, look forward at least 36 months and understand what expertise and leadership skills are required to accomplish your goals in the moment and in the future. Do not hesitate to initiate appropriate team changes to maintain focus and employee morale.

It's All About Me

DR. PAUL BATES

aul has worn many hats from entrepreneur in the financial marketplace to consultant, director, and academic. He has hired a multitude of staff. Paul's worst hire came during a time when he led a national financial services firm, and he was searching for the next leader of a growing sales division.

Paul recognizes that there are unique issues that surface when hiring sales professionals compared to other personnel within the company. "There is a delicate balance between the skills you are searching for and the candidate's self-pride, confidence and self-entitlement mindset that some strong sales leaders possess." Looking back on this costly hiring mistake, Paul clearly remembers the candidate indicating to the team that he would be "indispensable" to the company if he were hired. The candidate was very focused on "self" using the terms "I" and "Mine," rather than the collective "We" and "Ours." The title of the role was also extremely important to the candidate.

This person had all the right credentials for the role but was focused on what he would gain from the business relationship with, apparently, little regard for the company or the team members. His attitude and mindset were extremely self-centered, and while Paul and the team observed glimpses of these attitudes in the interview, they neglected to act on them. The hire was made and Paul quickly found out that when the new hire travelled, he would only stay at the best hotels and dine at expensive restaurants. He also requested frequent meetings to discuss increasing his compensation plan. The sales team observed this mindset and behavior and were patiently waiting to see what would be done about this manager's self- serving attitude and tendency towards personal gain compared to team contribution. The team was suffering. While this individual had several strong skills, there was no opportunity to reassign him to a role as a sole contributor, thus Paul had to part ways with the employee.

COST:

Hard cost $150,000 to $200,000,
Real Costs: substantial.

PAUL BATES

Dr. Paul Bates MTS, DPT, FCPA, FCMA, CMC has served with a number of companies in the Canadian capital markets sector. Paul has held the President's office at four major brokerage and investment firms and also successful start-ups. Paul is a highly-rated speaker in the areas of leadership, ethics, strategy, conflict resolution, innovation, financial management and entrepreneurship.

Keep an eye out for the words candidates use in the interview. Are they all about themselves, or do they use words that indicate a team mindset? If the hire is for a management role, monitor to see if the conversation is about helping others or their own personal gain. One key indicator might be their focus on compensation.

The Intimidation Factor

BRADEN DOUGLAS

Braden is the Founder of CREW, an award-winning marketing agency providing complete marketing solutions (strategy and execution). Braden speaks at events to audiences across North America and around the world and writes regularly through social media and online.

Over the years Braden has hired over 100 business professionals in his business and through managing other teams. His worst hire was a director of marketing for his company CREW. Getting this hire right was critical as the role required the manager to maintain solid business relationships with clients while managing a team of marketing professionals. As with many bad hires, Braden was desperate to fill the role as quickly as he could.

A candidate had been referred to Braden by a respected past employee, and Braden assumed the candidate would be competent and qualified for the role. Braden admits that because this person was coming from a well-branded and larger company, he was intimidated by the candidate's background. Braden was afraid of insulting the candidate, so he did not ask them to complete one of the standard case studies that the company would typically use to qualify a candidate's work before they were hired. There was no formal interview, and a much higher than normal salary was offered to the candidate as added incentive.

Red flags went up immediately due to the new director's lack of computer skills, inability to think strategically on client projects and lack of required detail. The new hire simply was not used to doing the hands-on work. Within six months staff were beginning to leave and clients were complaining. To top it off, a fellow CEO heard Braden had hired the new director and commented that he knew of the person and was surprised Braden would have brought him on board. A formal improvement plan was put in place with the new hire, he rejected it and promptly quit.

COST:

Mental anguish and over $350,000.

BRADEN DOUGLAS

Braden Douglas is the Founder of CREW Marketing Partners, one of Canada's largest agencies specializing in Food & Beverage. After a BBA from Laurier, Braden started his career in brand management at Frito Lay and Procter & Gamble. Braden is also a professional speaker, author, and blogger at bradendouglas.com and lives outside Vancouver, British Columbia, with his wife and two kids.

Be careful not to be too impressed by a candidate's experience or intimidated by their past qualifications. Treat every candidate equally by using the same assessment process. If you have a hiring process that requires candidates to complete a simulation or work sample assignment, don't think anyone is above the required task. Truly qualified candidates will welcome the due diligence.

Putting Family First

BOB YOUNG

Bob is the founder of Lulu.com and co-founded RedHat, the open source software company. He is also owner of the CFL Hamilton Tiger Cats. Bob's track record of success is evident but he, like so many, had to start somewhere and with few financial resources. His worst hire will be appreciated by anyone who is in business with family members—specifically a spouse.

Bob's worst hire involved the need for a COO for his newly formed start-up. A lack of capital, coupled with the need to hire someone more organized than himself, formed the foundation for the search. Bob is your typical entrepreneur; he has the vision and ability to sell investors and clients on his offering but lacks organization and follow through, thus the need for this role to be delegated to someone more skilled in these areas. Bob searched the market, but ultimately the only person he could afford at the time was his wife. Bob's wife was extremely competent in the role and proved efficient in keeping Bob organized. However, having his wife in the role of COO took a toll on their marriage. Bob's wife was working in the business as well as working in the home and raising three young children. As Bob remembers, "When you and your spouse work together, it is almost impossible to leave the business at the office. You typically bring it home, and it becomes a 24/7 business relationship."

This worst hire experience motivated Bob to pursue the business' success so he could hire someone to replace his wife and get his personal life back on track. That is exactly what happened, and eventually Bob was able to bring a new COO onboard. This hire taught Bob a personal lesson that goes far beyond business success—the value of a successful and happy family.

COST:

A very unhealthy work/home
relationship with his wife.

BOB YOUNG

Bob is Founder of self-publishing company Lulu.com, and co-founded Red Hat, the open source software company. He was named one of the "Top 50 Agenda -Setters in the Technology Industry in 2006" and was ranked as the fourth "top Entrepreneurs for 2006" both by Silicon.com. He is also caretaker of the CFL's Hamilton Tiger-Cats football club.

Don't allow your business goals
to get in the way of what is really
important—family. There is stress in
both areas of life, work and marriage,
so do your best to ensure you
protect them both. If you can, hire
from outside of your family, and leave
the family as priority #1"!

The Unseen Deal Breakers

CHIP WINCHELL

C hip is a perfect example of someone who is sold on the company he works for, so much so that he bought the company. He has hired hundreds of people in his career, most of them being profitable hires. Chip's worst hire came through the referral of a candidate who had previously turned down Chip's offer of employment.

Chip was in dire need of a senior sales representative in a profitable region of the country. The hiring team had put out the feelers to the market to search for candidates and the search seemed to be on track until the #1 candidate turned down their offer. The team went from excitement to panic overnight. The territory needed someone in the role ASAP, and they didn't have any candidates. The coveted #1 candidate who had turned down the offer contacted Chip with a referral. The fact that the new candidate had been referred by the top most qualified candidate inspired the team to rush the interview, neglecting to explain some of the key requirements of the job, not the least of which was a requirement of 2 to 3 days of overnight travel per week in the territory. Travel meant that the salesperson would typically be driving from one city to another in the early evening, thus arriving when it was dark. The offer was made and accepted. All was going well until the candidate was informed of the required 2 to 3 nights per week evening travel. For most salespeople this would not be an issue but in this particular instance, the new sales person had night vision problems and was unable to drive in the dark which obviously caused significant appointment scheduling challenges. After a few months the candidate refused to travel and resigned leaving Chip frantically searching for a new salesperson and having to start the search all over again while losing profitable selling time in the territory.

COST:

$350,000, plus lost sales revenue while the territory was open.

CHIP WINCHELL

Chip Winchell is CEO at CableServ Inc., where he previously held the positions of Senior Vice President and Vice President of Sales. Chip holds a Bachelor of Science in Communication Media from the State University of New York, Fredonia with concentrations in broadcast and human communication.

Candidates need to understand all requirements of the job—specifically the expected amount of travel and related expense policies. A candidate should never be left with assumptions of the role when they accept an offer of employment. Details that employers think are not significant can be deal breakers for candidates. Don't assume anything!

The Insight of a Roleplay

GORDON STEIN

Gordon understands hiring! Gordon estimates that he has been involved in over 2000 interviews and was instrumental in growing a staffing firm from $6 million to $150 million in revenue with a simple formula—hire great people!

The majority of Gordon's hires have been in revenue generating roles and he freely admits that he has made some bad hires. His worst hire lasted less than a day due to the fact that the role required regular air travel. Turns out that this rather relevant tidbit of information wasn't adequately addressed during the interview. Who would have thought that a candidate would accept a role requiring 50% travel time when they had a fear of flying?

The new hire had a phobia of flying and rather than facing their fears the employee simply called Gordon and quit on the spot. As Gordon states, "You have to face the fact that you are dealing with people, and sometimes they simply surprise you!"

Gordon knows his worst hire is an interesting story but he was keen to share with the reader his formula for success when hiring sales people.

Therefore, Gordon's nugget is not related to the story we have just told you. His mantra is, "Don't waste a seat with someone that is not incredible." When hiring salespeople, his success boils down to a simple process during the interview. "Let's do a roleplay!" Immediately upon making that statement, Gordon will look right into the candidate's eyes and wait for their reaction. The candidate will either freeze in their tracks or lean forward and engage. For those keen to engage, a further confirmation of their fit into the company would be how they perform during the roleplay and their willingness to receive input and then incorporate those ideas into the role. "A simple roleplay will quickly show you if they are a natural or if they simply talk a good game."

COST:

Interview time of management and time to source, assess and hire new person

GORDON STEIN

Gordon Stein's career includes increasingly senior roles as a sales, marketing and operations executive at companies including IBM, Dell, Rogers and Apple. He is the author of Cashflow Cookbook, a different kind of personal finance book that helps people build wealth with minimal effort and sacrifice. Gordon is now a professional speaker. He holds an Engineering degree from Western University and an MBA from the Rotman School of Business.

Use simple roleplays or simulations to force the candidate to show what they know and how they engage in different business settings. If you see that they shy away (specifically if it is in a client engagement role), be careful. Listen to what they tell you in the interview and compare it to what you see in the roleplay!

The Brilliant Jerk

MARK BACHMAN

Mark's worst hire is one that he likes to call the "Brilliant Jerk" employee, someone who excels in one particular function of the job but is incompetent in other key factors of the role or following company protocol.

Mark has been challenged in hiring this type of employee a few times, specifically in his channel management department, where the role requires his sales channel team to support the channel. The short-term requirement of the job is for the channel manager to have a hunter mindset for the main purpose of acquiring new business channel partners, the second and more challenging element of the role is the ongoing channel relationships. Mark realizes there is a dilemma for this type of hiring, as it is difficult to acquire an equal mix of both required skills in one person. The issue for Mark was putting too much weight on the hunter mindset of the candidate and less on the candidate's desire to manage partnership relationship.

In Mark's worst hire, The Brilliant Jerk Channel Manager knew she was a highly skilled and talented salesperson and believed she could build better relationships with clients than the channel partners themselves. This newly hired salesperson decided to ignore the company channel procedures training she had received and bypass the channel partners and go directly to the client. Rather than building strong lasting relationships with the channel, she was building up walls and causing significant problems internally and outside the company. There was no denying that the new hire was a "Brilliant" salesperson but to the channel and internal support staff she was constantly causing relationship problems. To save existing business relationships the Channel Manager was released.

COST:

Damage to Channel Partnership and around $200,000 in lost revenues.

MARK BACHMAN

Mark is a Co-Founder and CEO of FlipGive, a team funding app that helps families raise money for their kid's activities. FlipGive has helped over 50,000 teams, groups and organizations across North Americaraise more than $25 million by simply leveraging their everyday spending. He also co-founded Better The World Inc. and Prolink Consulting Inc. He lives outside Toronto with his wife and 3 kids who participate in multiple sports and community activities. Mark holds a BA and MBA from Ivey School of Business at Western.

Manage the risk of hiring a Brilliant Jerk by assigning weights to different functions of the job and assessing the candidate against each of these weights. A candidate may excel in a lower weighted or short-term activity, but they must be as strong in the higher weighted long-term elements of the role.

What You Cannot Test For

JAMES PETERS

James is Chairman of Hadrian Manufacturing. The company, named after the Hadrian Wall, highly values its culture, and James believes one of his main jobs is to build a protective wall around the highly valued culture his team has built over the years.

James' story is about a candidate slipping past the hiring guards of the company fortress through great interview skills and a highly accomplished financial acumen. What was overlooked during the hiring process, however, was the ability to judge the candidate's lack of perspective concerning work and staff. As James remembers, this lack of perspective slowly chipped away at the company culture within the finance team. The manager was as equally concerned about a penny missing as a million dollars. Team members were being run over by a hardnosed, inflexible manager who continually put results above internal staff relationships. Statements balanced to the penny and on a rigid timeline completely outweighed the treatment of staff in a manner that James and his senior management team prided themselves on. The fortress had been penetrated and the finance work environment had turned toxic.

James and his team knew within a very short time period that a hiring mistake had been made but the company was on an upward growth curve and the reporting from the new manager was meeting acute needs. Looking back the senior management team sacrificed long term health within their company culture for short term expediency. James believes coaching is all about taking a good employee and making them better, and coaching was simply not an option for this individual. The manager was set in their ways and needed to exit the company.

COST:

Credibility in the eyes of the company.

JAMES PETERS

James is Executive Chair of the Hadrian Group of Companies. Prior to this he was President of Hadrian from 1997-2017. James is also Chair of Formula Solutions Inc. and is on the boards of IJM and Young Life. James is a Charter Director and has an MBA from McMaster University and an HBSCF from Lakehead University.

Technical skills are a given. You can test for these skills but what you can't test for is the way new managers will treat your valuable team members. Act swiftly and decisively when a new or existing manager's actions are degrading your culture. Don't think it will get better—it won't.

Don't forget the Criminal Record Check

KIM ADES

Kim is a well-known and respected coach to senior business professionals. Before she moved into her coaching business, she had a successful company selling services and technology to the marketplace.

Kim's worst hire is one that makes you shake your head and say "Wow—how did that happen?" Kim was a young business owner, occupied with growing her company and she recognized that the sales team could use a more experienced, seasoned sales professional who could open up accounts in larger organizations. Kim determined that this new sales hire would be beneficial in teaching her and her young team sales processes and other related knowledge that the company was currently lacking. Kim's number one goal was to hire a professional who would bring a level of sales maturity and credibility into the pursuit of high-level sales opportunities. After posting online and sorting through dozens of resumes Kim short listed a few candidates and interviewed them to the best of her abilities.

Kim narrowed it down to what she considered to be the best candidate for the job and sealed the hire. Everything was going great. Kim invested in the purchase of a new computer for the seasoned senior sales hire, spent a good deal of time training on the service offering, and then immediately moved the candidate into selling. Much to everyone's surprise, this new hire made a sale to a brand-new client within the first three weeks of being employed. Kim thought she had hit the jackpot. The following Monday however, she was feeling quite the opposite. Over the weekend, the new hire had cleared out their desk, taken the newly purchased laptop with them and on top of that had used and maxed out the new client's credit card on a weekend shopping spree. No resignation letter and Kim has never been able to locate the dishonest salesperson or recoup any of her losses.

COST:

Immediate loss of the new client and Kim's lost confidence in hiring new staff.

KIM ADES

Kim Ades is the President and Founder of Frame of Mind Coaching™ and JournalEngine™ Software. Kim is recognized as an expert in the area of thought mastery and mental toughness, to help business owners and leaders identify their personal blind spots and shift their thinking in order to yield extraordinary results. Author, speaker, entrepreneur, coach, and mom of five, Kim's claim to fame is teaching her powerful Frame of Mind Coaching process to executives, entrepreneurs, and leaders world-wide.

For any young hiring managers, it is always wise to have a set of experienced eyes (internal staff or outside consultants) in the interview process with you to assist in assessing candidates. Don't let age or inexperience stop you from digging deeper into a seemingly more mature, experienced candidate's background or from conducting a criminal check.

Sometimes You Get What You Pay For

JAMIE CARDELLA

As a young entrepreneur, Jamie began his career building a consulting company prior to entering the general insurance world.

Jamie clearly remembers his worst hire a few years back when the division he was running had a need for additional sales talent. Jamie's budget only allowed for one hire, so he needed to get the hire right the first time.

In one of the interviews, Jamie started to ask some tough questions around this candidate's business network. The candidate's responses seemed a little vague, so Jamie dug deeper into the "network" question, but the responses remained shallow and irrelative. Jamie was unable to go any further because at that very moment another member of the interview team jumped in to ask a question regarding compensation and the candidate's expected base salary. To everyone's surprise, the candidate's salary requirement was the lowest of all the shortlisted candidates. The mood of the interview turned on a dime and Jamie could see that the team was more interested and excited about the candidate's underbudget compensation requirements than his responses to their interview questions.

Jamie took a quick look into the candidate's LinkedIn profile and noticed only 20 LinkedIn contacts listed. Red flags were raising for Jamie, but the other executives were determined to make the hire based primarily on the candidate's base salary level. The hire was made, and within the first 90 days Jamie knew it was a major mistake. The candidate basically had no business network. The team gave the new hire all the chances in the world but had to release them after 9 months of lost revenue opportunities from the client base.

COST:

Opportunity cost extrapolated over expected revenue lost is over $2 million.

JAMIE CARDELLA

Jamie Cardella is President of divisions for HUB Ontario and also serves as a member of HUB's Executive Team. Prior to HUB, Jamie was an owner of Sinclair-Cockburn Insurance Brokers, a successful venture that eventually saw a sale to HUB in 2010. Jamie has been selected as a top 40 under 40 executives, has written for several publications and is a noted speaker for varied risk management engagements. Prior to insurance and during his early twenties, Jamie built and eventually sold a sales and marketing firm with a business partner.

It is tempting to be attracted to a candidate with a lower compensation requirement compared to other candidates. Try to keep compensation out of the discussion until you know the candidate is competent and capable of excelling in the specific role.

A Good Way To Lose A Friend

BRIAN MCCARTHY

Brian didn't hesitate for a moment when asked to describe his worst hire. The first words out of his mouth were "I lost my best friend when I hired them!" This is a painful story for Brian but a great learning nugget for all of us in a hiring capacity.

Brian remembers meeting his friend on the street and realizing something was terribly wrong. This friend and his spouse had lost their jobs on the same day and they were deeply concerned about their financial future. At the time, Brian was running his own company and had the freedom to make quick decisions so he immediately asked his friend if he would like to work with him in his growing business. Rather than parking the friendship and the emotional tug of wanting to help them out, and treating his friend like any other hire, Brian invited them to his office to discuss a position that didn't even exist in the company. Brian was doing a friend a favour, but unfortunately that favor quickly turned into an expensive nightmare.

Brian didn't want to get into the many painful details of this story and what went wrong in the hire, but felt the reader could be warned about avoiding this type of terrible hiring mistake. As Brian says, "I thought I knew this friend, but I realize now that I had no idea who they would be as an employee in my business. I should have had other team members interview and assess my friend's business acumen and capabilities." Up until the time of this hire Brian had always followed a logical and clearly defined hiring process. In this instance, however, Brian let personal emotion take the place of logical thinking by side stepping due diligence because it was his friend.

COST:

Lost personal friendship which no money can replace. Plus $100,000 in hard costs

BRIAN MCCARTHY

Brian McCarthy has been leading sales teams in various industries for 25 years. He has been CEO of his own firm and with over 200 hires he has learned the hard way of what difficulties a poor hire does to an organization. Specializing in the insurance brokerage world where sales cycles can be complex and technical, Brian has become a believer in aptitude testing and simulations before hires.

One of the best ways to lose a good friend is to hire them and have them report to you. What you know about a personal friend may be different from what they are capable of delivering in business. Paint everyone with the same brush.

The Jekyll and Hyde Candidate

MARK WHITTEN

As CEO and President, Mark has been personally involved in over 100 key, strategic hires during his career.

His worst hire revolves around the recruitment and hiring of a human resource manager for one of his largest facilities. In this particular facility Mark and his senior management team had worked tirelessly restoring trust throughout the plant and front office due to past issues. His new HR manager would be responsible for enhancing, nurturing, and maintaining this critical trust culture.

Within six short weeks of the new HR Manager joining the company, Mark started getting hints from the shop floor and front office staff that the new HR manager was not the "Trust Minded Ambassador" he was hoping for. Mark met with different teams to hear their perspective, and he learned that they had a Jekyll and Hyde manager on their hands. The HR manager said all the right things in management meetings, but when it came time to manage and deal with employees, their actions bordered on being cruel and mean spirited. These destructive actions were never displayed in view of the team but behind closed doors in individual meetings. After confrontation and unsuccessful attempts to coach this HR Manager, Mark ultimately had to terminate the employee. Regretfully, one of Mark's most valued employees resigned prior to the termination due to the mistreatment they had endured.

Within a few weeks the fired Manager attempted to sue the company. As Mark found out later, this employee had been fired for similar reasons in the past and had unsuccessfully attempted to sue two of their last employers.

COST:

Lost key employee, time required to rebuild trust in the company, credibility in the eyes of the employees, and a minimum of $150,000 in soft and hard costs.

MARK WHITTEN

Mark is President & CEO of Spartanburg Steel Products in Spartanburg, South Carolina. His career has spanned the heavy truck and automotive market in Canada, Mexico and the United States. In 2017 he started sharing his message on servitude leadership, employee engagement and culture through conferences and contributing articles to IndustryWeek magazine. Throughout his career, he has witnessed firsthand the power of an engaged workforce, and the resulting correlation to overall business results.

Don't rely on what you see and hear
in an interview. Use behavior-based
scenario questions to attempt to uncover
how your valuable team members
will be treated by a new leader. Trust
the tools to drive the right questions.
Check references and do your due
diligence with respect to background
checks and employment history. This
will give you the best opportunity to
uncover any flaws and expose potential
cracks in a candidate's fabric.

Don't Forget the Employment Agreement

BOB REMINGTON

B ob started a distribution business right out of college and has successfully managed and grown his profitable company since 1983. From inception, Bob's goal has been to meet the needs of his employees and clients. As Bob found out in one of his senior hires within his company, being too generous, specifically with legal employment contracts, can come back to haunt you.

At the time of Bob's worst hire, the company was growing, and he was doing a lot of traveling. There was a need for him to hire an executive that could take over some of his operational, marketing, and sales management functions. Bob knew of a well-qualified individual from his past and approached them to consider an opportunity to work with his team. Interviews and references were done, and all was going well until the employment agreement required signing from both parties. The candidate had inserted a few final changes to the contract, including a high buyout clause if the candidate's employment was ever terminated. At first, Bob resisted but his schedule was full and he needed to get this person on board. Since the company was profitable and the candidate and Bob got along so well Bob finally gave into the one-sided employment demands and signed the agreement.

All was going well for the first year, but then Bob started to hear of complaints from his employees of the heavy-handed management style being used, specifically when Bob was out of the office travelling. Within a short time, a few of Bob's key staff members quit and the new senior executive was losing their enthusiasm for the job. Bob needed to act, but his hands were tied on account of the "exit clause" in the employment agreement. The cost of terminating the executive significantly delayed Bob's decision and ultimate action of terminating the executive, causing unrest with the team and a significant slowdown in the company's growth plans.

COST:

Between $3,000,000 and $4,000,000 in missed growth plus credibility with team.

ROBERT REMINGTON

Robert is CEO of Remington Medical where he started his medical company in 1983 after graduating from BCIT in Vancouver, Canada. Over the years Remington Medical has been providing innovative and exclusive medical products primarily to the rehabilitation markets. Their company mantra is "Help Canadians Get Better Faster."

An employment contract is like a marriage, there is a cost to getting out of the relationship. The interview stage is like a date and all you are seeing and experiencing is the good side of the candidate. Replace your emotions with logic when designing your employment package, just in case the relationship takes a turn.

What Didn't You Say?

DON LEVY

D on is a senior financial planner, investment advisor, and portfolio manager. He has operated and owned his own business for 27 years. Don believes that as an advisor, it's important to have a strong moral compass that directs you to do the right thing for your clients. However, it is another thing to actually find and hire advisors that meet and exceed your ethics and high moral standards. Don prides himself on how he has been able to attract and hire talent that fits effortlessly into his business and has gained insights about the hiring process from past challenges.

Don's worst hire took place many years ago when hiring an associate advisor for his team. At the offer stage of the hiring process, Don asked for current references but was not given one from the candidate's most recent employer. Rather than call older references, Don took it on himself to reach out to the most recent employer and was met with a well scripted response. It was impossible to get any substantial information from the reference. Rather than picking up on the clue, Don called the other references provided by the candidate and finally made the hire.

This new advisor was very good at bringing in new business and seemed to have a smooth tongue that convinced clients to trust them, but just six months later, Don was hearing complaints from staff concerning this advisor's complete lack of ethics. Colleagues claimed that they habitually misrepresented the truth to clients. After approaching the advisor about these concerns, Don was informed by a client that the advisor had breached the ethics protocol. Don terminated the advisor immediately. However, the advisor systematically harassed and attempted to discredit Don for months.

COST:

Reputation with clients, legal fees, and significant personal stress caused by repeated harassment from the dismissed employee.

DON LEVY

Don is the Managing Director of the Confido Wealth Team at Manulife Securities Incorporated. As well as running his own business, Don has been a senior financial planner, investment advisor and portfolio manager. He is a fellow of the Canadian Securities Institute (FCSI) having completed several professional designations including certified financial planner (CFP), chartered investment manager (CIM) and trust and estate practitioner (TEP). His investment principles are rooted in proven wealth creation strategies, and great client service is of paramount importance to him.

No candidate should be given
serious consideration for a role until
all steps of the hiring process are
completed. This includes speaking to
a recent employer, especially if the
candidate is unemployed. Sometimes
what a reference does not say may
be the information you are looking
for. Park your emotions until you have
all the facts.

The Finger Pointing Candidate

DEBBIE MCGRATH

D ebbie is known and very well respected throughout the world as a leader in HR knowledge and content. However, like other leaders, she is still susceptible to making costly hiring mistakes.

It was easy for Debbie to follow the thread of what she recognized in her past worst hires, "I am a sucker for a sob story!" In the case of one of these hiring mistakes, Debbie had been contacted by a business associate who was trying to help a friend whose whole world seemed to be falling apart. Debbie's immediate response was to find a way she could help this poor soul. Debbie brought them in for an interview for a job she felt might be a good stepping stone to them get back on her feet. The interview consisted of listening to all the terrible things that had been happening to the candidate and how everyone in their life had been mistreating them.

As the saying goes, when you point one finger at another person you have three pointing back to you. It seems that the real problem was the candidate and not the people they were blaming. Evidence of this occurred pretty much the moment this new candidate joined Debbie's company. Working three months with this person was enough time for the team to understand why the new hire had so many problems in their life; they were a master of the "Blame Game." The role was a train wreck due to their negative talk and inability to get along with team members and clients. Debbie had to release the new hire.

COST:

The biggest personal cost was the relationship between the person who referred the candidate to Debbie. To the company, it was detrimental to client relationship and lost sales opportunities.

DEBBIE MCGRATH

Debbie is Chief Instigator HR.com. Community Builder, Tech entrepreneur, HR enthusiast. HR.com is the largest destination site for HR Executives and touches over 1,000,000 HR professionals each month. She is a mother of 5, a slow sloppy skier and bad red wine drinker.

Monitor the words candidates use in their speech when talking with you and others in an interview. Do they complain about past employers or blame others for past failures? Ask questions to find out if they are willing to take responsibility for their own actions and admit mistakes or whether they point fingers at others.

Like Ripping Off A Bandage

BRIAN MCLAUGHLIN

B rian has been involved in over 200 mid to senior level hires in his career and views hiring as an eye-opening experience, both positively and negatively.

The HR group that Brian was leading at the time of his worst hire was new and needed to gain credibility and acceptance by the head office and branch personnel. The jury was still out with the executive team on the need to expand this HR division, so proving their worth to the company was essential. It was in this business setting that Brian found himself making his worst hire. The role in question was a director to meet the HR needs of head office and the branch network across the country.

Throughout the interview Brian emphasized the need for his director-level team members to lead by example in the way they conducted their business. Brian noticed approximately two weeks after hiring his new director that they were consistently arriving to work 1 to 1.5 hours late and leaving with everyone else at 5PM. Brian wasn't the only one in the office to notice this activity but he gave it a week before having a chat with the new Director. The new hire explained that they had some logistic difficulties in the morning, so Brian and the new director agreed to move their starting time up an hour and add that hour to the end of the day. It wasn't two weeks into the newly agreed upon starting time that the Director started arriving an hour late. Over the next two months, Brian had to sit-down and continually remind the Director that their actions were setting the wrong tone and making the HR team look bad in the eyes of management. No matter what the candidate said they would do to correct the "arriving late" issue, things never changed. Brian dismissed the new hire at the 60-day mark of their employment.

COST:

Department reputation was damaged, branch network suffered and financially over $100,000 hard costs.

BRIAN MCLAUGHLIN

Brian McLaughlin is CHRO of McKesson Canada. McKesson Corporation is a top 5 Global company focusing on the health care industry. Brian has held senior HR leadership roles at Rexall Pharmacy Group, Katz Group, TD Bank and Canada Trust. Over his career he has been involved with mergers, acquisitions, divestitures and other strategic business opportunities. Brian holds a degree from University of Toronto, majoring in Commerce and Economics.

Don't think you have the ability to change every new hire's bad habits or behaviors. When you spot bad behavior and the new hire doesn't respond to repeated coaching or advice, you need to realize you have made a hiring mistake and release the person immediately. Like taking off a bandage—it has to be done quickly! Everyone suffers with delayed action.

Do Not Assume Anything

GERRY O'MAHONEY

During his career, Gerry has grown teams from 6 members to 2,500 strong in as short a period as 3 years. Bottomline, Gerry knows hiring!

As a senior director at one of North America's largest financial institutions Gerry ran his schedule at break neck speed with continuous back-to-back meetings and no time for any admin of the business. Gerry was allowed this gift of productivity and operations running smoothly due to his exceptional EA. Unfortunately, this person was set to leave the role and the hunt was on for a replacement of equal excellence and value. This was the one area where Gerry could not afford to make a mistake, and here is the story of his worst hire.

A short list of highly qualified candidates was selected, and Gerry and the team honed in on a candidate who was very professional, articulate, well dressed, and highly recommended. After two weeks on the job, the newly hired EA came into Gerry's office telling him that they needed to hire an EA to assist them in their role. They simply could not keep up to Gerry's hectic pace of work and schedule. Hiring another assistant to be Gerry's assistant's assistant was out of the question.

As Gerry reflects on this mis-hire, he is acutely aware of the mistakes that were made. During the interview, Gerry and the team spent too much time on the candidate's skills and past experience, and they very little time informing the candidate of the high demands of the role due to Gerry's frantic and extremely busy schedule. This candidate was set up for failure since they had no idea what they were getting themself into. They lasted a mere two weeks and this caused a complete slowdown in Gerry's and the team's schedule for many months afterwards.

COST:

Significant financial cost to the department, Gerry's ego and pride were crushed.

GERRY O'MAHONEY

Gerry has spent his career in Financial Services from Branch Banking, Technology roles, Brokerage, Mutual Funds, Foreign Exchange, Treasury & Investments. He is a C-Suite executive with a track record of building and enhancing complex technical infrastructure that support clients in different regulatory environments around the globe, both online and in face to face delivery channels. He has also participated in a number of due diligence exercises in both acquisitions and disposals.

Do not assume candidates understand the complexity, time commitment or what the team's definition of "busy" is within the role. What may seem routine to you may be completely over the candidate's head. You need to have a clearly articulated picture of the job, the required expectations, and not be afraid to paint a realistic picture for clarity!

Giving Lip Service to The Hiring Process

LYELL FARQUHARSON

Lyell began his career in the public accounting sector where he had the good fortune to be responsible for recruitment. This hiring experience laid a solid foundation for hiring throughout his career.

His worst hire took place when he was running an organization and needed to fill the executive HR role. Due to the nature of the role, he instinctively knew he may not see any signs of a hiring mistake for a minimum of 6 to 9 months so he was adamant that he be personally involved and active in this critical hire. Lyell's executive team was made up of high performing professionals, and they needed this new senior HR executive to add value to and complement an already strong team.

The challenge and ultimate hiring mistakes were two-fold. First, Lyell allowed his extremely busy schedule to take precedence over this critical hire. Secondly, he did not engage his executive team to assist in building out the key requirements of the senior HR role. In Lyell's mind, it was the perfect storm. Misguided priorities, a full schedule, and an unclear job description of the role.

Evidence of the bad hire showed up during the first executive roundtable meeting where the new VP of HR completely missed the mark during a presentation. Credibility was instantly lost with the executive team, and it was almost impossible to recover. From that point on the VP of HR and the team could not come together to make the cultural and team dynamics work cohesively. Lyell kept hoping for the best but after a year the candidate had to be asked to leave.

COST:

Executive management momentum and cohesiveness. Losses due to a poorly functioning senior management team.

LYELL FARQUHARSON

Lyell is an experienced Executive in the Travel and Airline business. He has worked with leading travel companies, WestJet as VP Global Sales, American Express Canada, as VP and GM., and Navigant and HRG as Canadian President, successfully leading these organizations through industry restructuring and the unprecedented events of 911, SARS, and Financial Crisis, that had profound impact on the Companies and industry. He is active on the Board of several Non-Profits and Board Member and Chair of Audit Committees for two Public Companies.

View your time spent on a senior
hire the way you would evaluate
and calculate the ROI of any other
investment in your company. Don't
give this level of a hire lip service and
then spend time on other projects
that don't have the same return or
potential damaging impact if the
decision is wrong.

Hiring from Outside
Your Industry

CHRIS LONG

C hris Long has a proven and successful track record of managing high performance teams in tier one financial services, government, healthcare, and major retail organizations.

Chris' worst hire took place when he was looking for a senior sales director to run a $100 million sales budget with a 35-person team. As Chris remembers, the hiring was simply taking too long. After a lengthy time interviewing many internal and external candidates, the team was wondering if they would ever find a candidate who would fit their specific requirements. The biggest requirement of the hire was to ensure instant credibility in front of both the company's internal stakeholder and the high demands of external clients. As Chris points out, "There is nothing worse than going to a meeting with your sales director, and they're like a deer in the headlights!"

A great candidate was identified, although it was noted that they had absolutely no industry experience. The candidate had interviewed well, but the focus zeroed in on their sales accomplishments with little regard to their ability or desire to learn the business. The struggle was real right from the start. The new sales director lacked the energy or ambition to educate themselves in the new industry and relied on team members to gird them up in client meetings. Before long the new hire was skipping industry events and backing away from client meetings. Chris spent time coaching the director, but it was like pushing a boulder uphill. Team members lost trust and confidence in the sales director and credibility with clients was starting to waver. The new Sales Director was released after much time and effort on Chris' part.

COST:

There were notable monetary costs, but Chris feels his own credibility with senior management peers and his team was lost.

CHRIS LONG

Chris is a Sales Vice President of Rogers Communications. Before joining Rogers, Chris was Head of Sales & Marketing with a Canadian IT Managed Services company. He earned Honours distinction in the Seneca Business Program while a member of the Varsity baseball and basketball teams. Chris continued his education with the Queen's University Executive Program.

There is nothing wrong with hiring from outside of your industry—in fact, this type of hire may bring fresh new ideas into the company. If the hire is from outside your industry and a key requirement is to learn your business, ensure you dig into their ability and desire to learn something new.

Listen to your Gut

DOREEN HARVEY

As one would expect of a senior HR professional, Doreen has experienced a few costly hiring mistakes in different roles during her successful career.

Doreen's worst hire involved a senior HR hire and ultimately impacted every department of the business. This is your classic "shoemaker's kids" story where HR is so wrapped up with HR initiatives throughout the company that they miss the mark in their own department. As Doreen states, "What you see and what you get can be completely different between the interview and when the candidate is actually on the job." For this hire, Doreen's team vetted a large number of resumes down to a short list, at which point the president and hiring team interviewed the candidates. The candidate that was selected had strong experience, said the right things in the interview, and looked the part. Doreen had an uneasy feeling concerning this particular candidate but could not put her finger on why. Because Doreen had no concrete evidence she could share with the President to back up her concerns, the team went ahead and made the offer, which was accepted.

The candidate was on the job no more than a few days before they transformed into a mean-spirited, aggressive tiger. The newly hired executive turned on a few key HR personnel and others behind closed doors. The image the president was seeing and what the HR team (and several members of the executive team) were experiencing was completely different which left those negatively impacted unable to provide defensible evidence of their concerns to the president. Since this was the head of HR, the positive culture within the company was quickly damaged. Doreen regretted not having administered any psychometric or personality tests that would likely have affirmed her gut feeling concerns.

COST:

Significant—over $1,000,000.

DOREEN HARVEY

Doreen has held senior positions in Human Resources with a multitude of industry leaders before establishing her own practice. Doreen is passionate about helping leaders work effectively with their people. She works closely with her clients to help align their human resources strategy to their business and organizational objectives. Doreen holds an MBA from the Schulich School of Business at York University and an HBA from Ivey.

If something does not feel right
and the cost of the hiring mistake
is significant, implement some
additional assessment tools
(Personality and Psychometric
Assessments) to provide datapoints
to assist you in formulating and
articulating your concerns. If you
have a concern, speak up and have
some form of data to back it up!

The Must-haves Before You Start the Search

TERRY HARNEY

Terry's story will hit home for anyone hiring a senior manager to run the day-to-day operations of a division or company.

Terry needed to free himself from these day to day operations, so he decided to hire a CEO for his business. Terry's strength was building their affiliate/partnership program, but there simply was not enough time in the day to do everything required. As Terry put it, "I was overwhelmed with too many projects on my plate and desperately required expertise I did not have in areas of the business that required attention." A trusted advisor noticed Terry's operations suffering due to his overloaded schedule and suggested a candidate who he believed could come in and run the operational side of the company. Due to the high recommendation Terry moved quickly and hired the candidate as CEO with little due diligence and no specifically defined job description.

Once the candidate started in the new CEO role, Terry

came to realize that what he thought he needed in a CEO compared to what the company actually required were two very different things. Rather than being freed up to focus on other matters, Terry was now constantly having to step in and fix problems. Both Terry and the new CEO were confused as to what exactly were their specific respective roles. Terry admits to flying blind in this critical hire, as he had not taken the time to clearly articulate what the company needed to complement his business strengths. This expensive mistake forced Terry to take a hard look at where he excelled and what he required in the new role. Terry dismissed the CEO and used his new knowledge and understanding to hire an outstanding CEO with clearly defined expectations.

COST:

$200,000 plus momentum in growth of business.

TERRY HARNEY

Terry Harney is the President and Founder of Synergy ECOHUB Solutions. The company is a project development firm focused on the conversion of MSW (garbage) to Hydrogen Gas. Mr. Harney worked in the industrial shredding market before founding Synergy and has extensive experience in the Waste Handling Field.

Don't even think of starting a search
until the team has defined, in clear,
explicit terms, what the company
wants and expects the successful
candidate to execute on. Have
a minimum of three skills and
competencies as must-haves and
use these as a base line for all of
your interviews and assessments.

The Job Hopper

CHRIS ASIMAKIS

Chris works under the philosophy that your hires will fall into the 10-80-10 rule. Of all the people you hire, 10 % will be stars, 80% will be average employees, and 10% will eat your valuable time and energy.

Chris' worst hire is one that stands out in his mind, because the writing was on the wall when he first reviewed the candidate's resume. Chris' initial thought was that the candidate was a "job hopper." The resume didn't lie. This candidate had too many jobs in a short period of time. That being said, with such a tight talent market, Chris and the team decided to go ahead and invite the candidate into the office for an initial meeting. It was clear that the candidate demonstrated good knowledge of the industry and presented well in the interview, however, Chris was still concerned about the number of jobs the candidate had had over the past ten years.

Unfortunately, the Engineer group needed to hire someone, and they had a candidate. The team bit the bullet, crossed their fingers, made an offer at the top of their compensation range, and hoped the hire would stick.

Not long into the hire the team realized why the candidate had so many jobs in a short period of time. This new hire was quickly fitting into the bottom 10%, and the team wanted him out ASAP. Chris thought maybe he could fit the candidate into another role in the company due to other hiring requirements at the time. Over a very short period of time, there were not one, but two departments that experienced the same costly bad hire with the same candidate, and Chris had to let the candidate go.

COST:

The organization and project suffered in multiple areas due to this poor hire.

CHRIS ASIMAKIS

Chris is an accomplished renewable energy executive. Chris is the Founder and Managing Director of Vassara Corporation. Prior to founding Vassara, Chris cofounded and was President and chief operating officer of Potentia Solar, which grew to become the largest rooftop solar company in Canada. At Enwave Energy Corporation, Chris was Chief Operating Officer and Executive Vice President of Business Development. Chris earned his MBA at University of Toronto's Rotman School of Management.

Let logic rule when hiring. If you suspect someone is a job hopper, do not ignore it. If there is a trend of job movement, do not think you will be any different. Use your head—if you have a concern regarding job movement get detailed reasons for each departure. Ask tough questions and get specific answers.

The Impact of a Hiring Decision on Your Team

ANDY AICKLEN

A ndy's career has allowed him to work with start-up dot.com firms to multi-national firms that have successfully gone public. He has worked with some of the most world-renowned brands in the technology sector. In one such company, sales grew from $250 million to over $1 billion in four short years. With this type of growth, Andy has witnessed the painful truth of costly hiring mistakes and how quickly candidates can come to be treated as commodities.

One experience in particular stands out for Andy as a turning point, where he determined from that day forward to always treat candidates and employees with the utmost respect. Andy would proudly say that he accomplished this over the years of running his own software distribution company, but that all changed when he decided to step away from the day to day operations and hire a general manager to run his business. Andy was happy to pass the baton on to his new hire and became so completely engrossed and focused on moving forward to his next new venture that he took his eye off the ball regarding the negative impact this move would have on his staff.

The new general manager's approach to business was so different to Andy's that the employees began to accuse Andy of abandoning them and the business. Andy admits that he talked himself into hiring the new general manager so he could get onto new, more exciting ventures, and also admits that he put little thought into the impact of this new hire. Suffice to say, the impact was immediate and adverse. The team felt that Andy was only looking after his own interests, not theirs, and they lost all the momentum they had built up. The business closed within the year.

COST:

Loss of respect of key employees, and ultimately the loss of his company.

ANDY AICKLEN

Andy Aicklen is a well-known technology executive and entrepreneur with over thirty years of experience in sales and leadership at companies such as Oracle, PeopleSoft, Hewlett Packard and Gartner Group. As Principal of Aicklen & Associates, he has worked with over 40 clients in North America, EMEA and Asia Pacific on a number of sales and leadership initiatives. Andy is a dual citizen of Canada and the US and earned his MBA at the University of Houston and a BA in Political Science from the University of Texas.

Hiring is not an isolated event. The ramifications of one hiring decision can impact every corner of the business. Hiring can easily become a selfish act of allowing the owner or manager to accomplish their personal goals at the cost of others. Before making a decision for your own self-interest, take a hard look at the impact the hire will have on your employee's lives!

A Walking Billboard

PATRICK LYNCH

P atrick is the recipient of many business awards in Ireland for the companies he has started. He is an author and speaker on the topic of entrepreneurship.

In any business community, reputation and brand recognition take years to build and must be guarded by all employees of the company. Patrick's worst hire, at first glance, is unique in that upon hearing about it, you might not think it would have such a significant impact on the hard-earned and very valuable brand recognition in his market. As Patrick states, "Every level of personnel within your firm is a walking billboard, and they have the ability to either increase or decrease the value of your brand in the public marketplace."

At the time of his worst hire, Patrick was operating a delivery business in southern Ireland. His highly visible branded delivery trucks, fitted with the company name and phone number, were used to deliver and pick up product from clients in different parts of southern Ireland. Those who drive the van in a professional manner go virtually unnoticed. Driven carelessly, a branding disaster is waiting for you around the next corner.

At the time, Patrick had not put too much thought into the drivers he hired. All he really needed to know was that they could drive his trucks and while doing so look adequately professional in the eyes of the client when delivering or picking up product. Poor and even reckless driving skills were not at the forefront of his mind as Patrick had never before received any complaints. Until, in the span of a short time, one bad driver had two major driving citations of driving over 100 KM in a 50 KM school zone. Not a good image for the company! Patrick worried first and foremost that someone was going to be hurt or even killed by this reckless driver, and secondly he worried how this was going to impact his company's image and reputation in the community. The driver had to be let go.

COST:

Mental anguish and unspoken diminished community branding.

PATRICK LYNCH

Pat Lynch is an Irish based serial entrepreneur, a business owner, angel investor, author, and a finalist in 2018 in the EY Entrepreneur of the Year. Pat is passionate about education and believes in sharing the business knowledge he has accrued through a lifetime of business experience and success.

If the candidate is one that will be in the public eye, your onboarding must ensure they understand that they are a walking billboard for the company. You must emphasize that their conduct is a reflection of the company. Also, any references should include a police check.

Ego and Pride Can Cost You

BRUCE ETHERINGTON

Bruce is known throughout the world as an international speaker and President of the Etherington Group. Due to Bruce's hectic travel and speaking schedule, his Executive Assistant is his most valued asset for his sanity and productivity. Bruce admits this worst hire story was all his fault.

A few years back, Bruce needed to hire a new EA. He had his team conduct a search and asked them to shortlist three candidates. Bruce met the short-listed candidates and with the team agreed that one of the EA candidates was a very good fit to work alongside Bruce. It was Friday, and the team was instructed to call the selected candidate on the following Monday and present the offer. That same Friday afternoon, Bruce received a call from an important client recommending someone they knew for what they assumed to be Bruce's open EA role. Not wanting to disappoint the client and neglecting to mention the fact that an offer was in the works and was to be presented the following Monday, Bruce agreed to meet the referred candidate that Saturday for coffee. After a casual meeting with this EA candidate,

Bruce informed his team Monday morning that he wanted to offer the job to the new candidate and for them to dismiss the one who was to receive the offer that very afternoon. The team was surprised and confused but went along with Bruce's decision.

The new hire showed up for their first day having little understanding of the company, the role, or exactly what the job entailed due to Bruce's short interview over coffee. After only 5 days on the job, Bruce arrived back to his office to find a resignation letter on his desk stating the role was completely over the EA's head. Their resignation left a gaping hole during an extremely busy time in the business.

COST:

Embarrassment and loss of credibility with team members, time to recruit, and the loss of the solid candidate who previously was to be hired.

BRUCE ETHERINGTON

Bruce is a renowned speaker and has addressed virtually every major insurance and financial planning organization in the world. His books "See the People" and "Reflect & Prepare" are international bestsellers, as are his CDs, which continue to change the lives of salespeople around the world. He is President of Bruce Etherington & Associates and is a fully accredited financial planner with a specialty in life insurance. Bruce holds the CLU, CHFC and CFP designations.

Don't allow pride or ego to get in the way of making wise hiring decisions. Your position should never allow you to bypass your team's due diligence and hard work in the hiring process. If hiring is not your strength, let others do it for you!

Admit Your Mistake and Act

CHRIS HEBB

C hris has a long and successful business track record in sports media (Orca Bay Sports Media & Entertainment and MLSE). Presently, he is the commissioner of the British Columbia hockey league.

Chris was Senior Vice President of one of the largest Sports and Entertainment media organizations in North America at the time of his worst hire. In his words, "In the Sports and Entertainment business, what takes place inside the sports complex and outside of the actual game is sometimes as important as the game itself." Many times during a professional basketball game, there is more entertainment off the court than what is taking place on the court with the players. A game entertainment manager is a key role and requires superior management skills and precise planning to pull these game entertainment elements off successfully.

At the start of a new professional basketball season Chris found himself without a game entertainment manager. The search went out, and the team quickly realized they weren't attracting anyone with the specific talent and skills required for the role. Under fire, a decision was made to hire and train a candidate who they thought had the potential to learn the role quickly and could then successfully lead the team. The manager was hired and a mere four weeks into the new role, not only did Chris know but his entire team knew that the hire had been a significant mistake. The new manager simply was not catching on and the paying fans ultimately were the ones paying the price. The ramifications of the mis-hire were so significant that Chris reacted immediately and terminated the relationship. It was extremely hard to terminate a new employee so quickly, but it was absolutely essential, and it was the right thing to do for all parties involved.

COST:

Poor fan experience in a professional sports entertainment business! Credibility lost at the executive level.

CHRIS HEBB

Chris is currently the Commissioner of the BC Hockey League and has spent a lifetime in sports. First as an athlete at the University of Victoria where the varsity basketball team captured the first of seven national collegiate championships in a row. Next, as a broadcaster, where he was a host/producer/reporter and received many honours for his work in documentaries. And, finally, as a pro sports executive with the Vancouver Canucks (NHL) and Grizzlies (NBA) and the Toronto Maple Leafs (NHL) and Toronto Raptors (NBA), where he oversaw the content divisions of the parent companies.

Be willing to admit you made a hiring
mistake and act quickly. In many
positions, waiting too long only adds
to the cost of the poor hiring decision.
No one wins when you try to hide
the hiring mistake—if you see the
mistake, everyone else does as well.
Deal with it quickly in a professional
and fair manner for all parties.

Clear and Concise Company Policies

RON FOXCROFT

R on is Chairman of Fluke Transportation and a legend in the N.C.A.A. basketball refereeing world. He is also the creator of the FOX 40 pealess whistle that is sold throughout the world.

Ron had a hard time picking his worst hire due to the many hiring mistakes he had experienced over the years. The one that stood out to him was a computer programmer who was able to pull the wool over Ron's eyes due to the company's lack of inhouse technical expertise. It seemed that at the end of the day the new hire always found a problem with the software that required them to stay late into the night to make the required system changes. At first, the executive team took these technical issues as legitimate system problems that required additional attention by the IT department. Eventually, it became clear that there was something amiss. Ron began to hear his team's misgivings about this employee, that perhaps they were not as aboveboard as everyone thought, but Ron didn't want to listen to their concerns due to the company's reliance on this person for technical support.

After more than a year of complaints by his staff, Ron was starting to become more concerned with the computer programmer's motives and integrity. Because this employee worked with sensitive company data, Ron decided to hire a private investigator. It didn't take them long to realize that the employee was misusing company time and resources. Ron immediately terminated the employee. A few months later Ron received a letter from the dismissed employee's lawyer claiming he was owed $50,000 in billable overtime. At first Ron thought it was more of a joke but that faded very quickly upon learning from his lawyer that Ron actually had no recourse due to the fact that there had been no policies in place defining what employees would and would not be paid for work that was completed outside of normal working hours.

COST:

Legal costs and settlement over $50,000 not including stress and time of management team.

RON FOXCROFT

Ron is an entrepreneur inducted into several business halls of fame and named Entrepreneur of the Decade by Profit Magazine. He is Chairman and CEO of Fluke Transportation Group Ltd. and Founder/CEO of Fox 40 International Inc. Ron is a recipient of the Order of Canada. Ron officiated the 1976 Olympic Gold Medal Basketball Game. In 2016, the National Association of Sports Officials (NASO) named Ron the recipient of the esteemed Gold Whistle Award, which is the officiating industry's highest honour bestowed on a referee.

Check and review your company policies and legal documents (or lack of them) to ensure you have covered the company from dishonest employees. An investment in a lawyer today is much less costly than using one to fight a disgruntled employee tomorrow.

Follow Your Gut to Know More

MARK WELCH

Mark is the author of The Street Savvy Sales Leader and past VP sales of some of the most progressive and innovative companies. Mark consults regularly with executive teams on sales strategy.

Mark's worst hire was with a newly created position within the company where he was senior VP sales and marketing. Up until this time, Mark was running the sales department but due to ongoing responsibilities, he needed to hire someone who would take over the sales team and report directly to him. The company was venturing into a new and profitable market and the opportunities were tremendous. Ensuring this new hire was able to execute in the role was critically important.

Everyone on the executive team knew the cost of making a mistake in this hire, but they quickly let their guard down once they met a candidate who "wowed the team" in the interview. Mark alone was hesitant as he felt the candidate was just a little too good in the interview. The other team members were sold on the candidate so Mark decided to keep quiet and let majority rule. The candidate was hired.

Things quickly turned sour. Trust amongst team members was immediately lost when the new hire brought in some of his own people whose main goal was to spy on other team members and report back to the new director. The high performing team pushed back, and before Mark knew it some of his key employees were taking stress leave and some of his most valuable team members were leaving the company and creating gaps that were almost impossible to fill. The culture changed so quickly it was impossible to fix and became the catalyst for Mark to leave the company as well.

COST:

Estimated in the millions.

MARK WELCH

Mark is the author of Street Savvy Sales Leadership, Certified Coach, Consultant and conference speaker. Mark has held leadership positions over his career and now consults with B2B firms to help them solve leadership challenges and specific sales related gaps, prioritize solutions, and execute to deliver breakthrough sales productivity results. Mark also coaches CEO's/Founders, Sales Manager's and Executive Sales Leaders to help them deliver the best results possible.

Your gut feelings are part of the hiring equation when evaluating candidates. Let the uneasy feeling be an indicator to push you to go deeper into knowing more about the candidate. If you feel other team members are missing something that you feel uneasy about, don't hesitate to speak up!

The Character Factor

MIKE O'LEARY

Mike is currently the president of Young Life Canada and has been involved in leadership roles in both the airline business and Young Life over the past 45 years. Mike has been involved in hundreds of hires over his career.

Mike's worst hire revolves around the concept that a person's character does not inherently improve with age. In Mike's case, he was hiring an area director and the candidate was someone he had supervised as a volunteer while the person was a university student. As Mike reflects on the story of his worst hire, he remembers that during their previous time together, the candidate had shown great promise but also some telltale signs of problematic character issues. As a young, relatively inexperienced manager, Mike wanted to believe that this candidate had matured and that bad behaviors in a working environment had been tamed. A resume showed that the candidate had been working with a reputable firm for the past five years and Mike took that as proof that somewhere along the way, rough edges had been worn down.

Unfortunately, it was not long after Mike hired this candidate that he recognized this was not the case. Bad habits had continued to flourish, and their impact was settling in and starting to contaminate the morale of coworkers within the division. Mike realized he put a risky apple in the barrel, and he needed to act. Mike has learned over the years that these types of hiring mistakes, left too long to fester, are difficult to terminate and costly in both time and money. "When the mission becomes too much a person than the mission itself, it is time to make a change." Termination of the employee was unpleasant and very costly.

COST:

Incalculable due to many factors that lasted years.

MIKE O'LEARY

Mike currently serves as President with Young Life of Canada in Vancouver, BC. He grew up and went to University in the Washington, D.C. area graduating with a B.S. in Journalism. Mike's career has been centered around Young Life over 40 years with a seven-year break in the middle as a project consultant and the duty manager of an airline ramp operation. He has an M.A. in theology from Fuller Seminary that has served him well in both secular and sacred management opportunities.

Character is an important bellwether for performance and an organization must weigh the cost of trying to wait out that kind of personal change in an otherwise talented person. If there are character flaws in your new hire, these flaws have the potential to impact your team environment. You need to see immediate, consistent positive change or act quickly and decisively to avoid a toxic work environment.

Set Up for Failure

CATHY HISCOTT

C athy's worst hire is one where she admits lack of communication to her team became the pivotal point where things went awry.

At the time of Cathy's worst hire, she was strategizing on how to assist her field managers in attracting and hiring quality sales professionals. Up until this point, the company had relied heavily on individual managers to conduct their own recruitment activities and hire their own field representatives. Her goal was to investigate and assess different methods of streamlining the current recruitment process. After much thought, Cathy's strategy was to centralize the recruitment activities and take some of the heavy lifting of hiring off the managers in the field. To accomplish this, she needed a new recruitment leader who would revamp the hiring process and run it centrally.

Cathy and her team began the recruitment and selection process to create a short list for the team to assess. The interview process included multiple interviews by different team members, one panel interview, and a case study to be completed by all candidates. After much time and effort by the team a decision was made on the candidate who excelled in all aspects of the hiring process. The failure in the hire had nothing to do with the mistake in the assessment of the candidate, but everything to do with the lack of preparation on Cathy's part to prepare the existing team for change. As a leader, Cathy was looking into the future while her team was looking at current needs. The newly hired recruitment leader was making strategic and tactical decisions based on Cathy's vision, and the team rebelled due in part to them not knowing why and where the new leader was taking the department. The new manager was caught in an internal battle that they did not want to fight and left the company.

COST:

Cathy's credibility with team.

CATHY HISCOTT

Cathy began her career as an advisor in 1991 with MetLife and since then has held numerous leadership roles in the exclusive and independent advisor network. Since joining FHG, Cathy has held the roles of; Vice President, Sales for the Ontario Region, President for the Ontario/Atlantic Region, and is currently the Sr. Vice President, Executive distribution officer, and President, Excel Private Wealth. Her team's mantra is "with you, for you".

When you are making changes
in strategy or direction within the
company or team, make sure your
team understands and is ready and
willing to accept the changes before
you hire anyone to lead the new
initiatives. If the team is not ready,
you will be setting your new hire up
for failure.

The Unpopular But Necessary Hire

DAVE HOOD

D ave's worst hire is especially interesting because he says he would do it all over again. He believes this bad hire was perceived with greater negativity from the eyes of his team, rather than from his own. Dave says, "There can be some small positive outcomes that result from a bad hire."

Dave's business was growing, had significant capital invested in new facilities, and had built a strong culture within the company. Dave was proud of the cultural mindset of his company and was looking for a senior leader who had proven technical skills along with a mindset that fit the company culture. After searching the market and not identifying any candidates who possessed both requirements, and due to their growth requirements, Dave's hand was forced into making the tough choice of favoring a candidate with technical skills over culture fit. To offset the concern, Dave offered the position to this candidate on a contractual basis rather than a full-time one. The contract was accepted, and the new senior manager came in and knocked it out of the park technically but failed miserably on internal relationships. Dave commented, "The new hire basically came in and swam against our cultural current but from a technical perspective, this is exactly what was needed at the time." Dave's biggest challenge and mistake was in not clearly communicating to the team that this decision was a short-term and painful process but was absolutely critical to future success. Dave and the team provided the senior leader constructive feedback concerning the culture/values gaps, but they simply did not have the experience to address these issues. The internal employees viewed this as a costly hiring decision, lacking in judgement, and from their perspective Dave's worst hire, but Dave considered it necessary to take this optics risk due to the critical technical needs of the company that no one else was able to provide. However, once the technical turnaround was completed, the senior manager's contract was terminated, and Dave immediately went to work on rebuilding trust within the team.

COST:

Created uncertainty and potential lost credibility in the eyes of team members that was hard to rebuild.

DAVE HOOD

Dave is an accomplished business leader with over 30 years of corporate, executive level experience in key leadership roles. In his roles as CEO and COO, Dave has been recognized for his ability to build successful and enduring businesses. In addition to building and scaling diverse companies, he has led and supported successful acquisitions and divestures. Dave has also contributed as a Director on Profit and Not for Profit Boards. Dave and his wife Susan live in Vancouver, BC and are the proud parents of three exceptional young adults. Dave holds an MBA from Athabasca University.

There will be times when hiring
decisions are required for the
survival of the company and will
be very unpopular with the team.
The key is communication! Make
sure your team knows why you
are making these hiring decisions,
and try to mitigate the damages by
reducing your exposure through
a contract rather than a full-time
agreement.

Decision-making When in Turmoil

LYNN HAZLETT

Lynn was the CEO of Primex Customs & Logistics at the time of her worst hire. Her company was recognized as one of the Top 50 fastest growing companies within 5 years of its inception.

Lynn's worst hire took place when she was expanding her business into the European marketplace. Lynn realized she could not manage the business from North America and required a leader with feet on the ground in Europe. The expansion into new geographical markets was extremely expensive and Lynn believed one of the best ways to attract the right talent was to offer equity incentives for the successful candidate, and she had to ensure she got the hire right the first time.

While Lynn was assessing candidates for the European expansion, she was also caring for her very ill mother and her time was split between the business and the hospital. Lynn's emotions were in turmoil, and she admits she was not thinking straight during a very stressful time in her life. Lynn had met a candidate who seemed to have most of what she was looking for in the role. Without a great deal of careful consideration, an offer was made, and the new hire began to implement a growth strategy of evaluating competitors that could potentially be valuable strategic acquisitions.

Difficulties arose seeing that the acquisitions were located in Europe while Lynn remained in North America coping with her ill mother. Pertinent information regarding business activities occurring overseas were not being accurately related to Lynn. Meanwhile Lynn had neglected to have a contract signed spelling out the boundaries of the business relationship with her new hire, due to her personal family situation. The new hire was able to move in to successfully acquire the competitor on their own and start a brand-new company leaving Lynn and her investors high and dry.

COST:

$6,000,000 and a lost business acquisition.

LYNN HAZLETT

Lynn was the Founder and CEO of Primex Customs & Logistics, a fully integrated international logistics company via airfreight, ocean, rail, trucking and warehouse distribution. From starting her company in her living room, Primex was selected as one of the top 50 fastest growing companies. Lynn successfully sold her business and has concentrated her time supporting start-up and midsize global organizations in strategy and growth. Lynn has been named in the Top 100 Business Women in Canada numerous times.

When you find yourself in emotional turmoil due to personal or business trauma—you need to step back and ask yourself if it may not be the right time for you to be making significant business investments or hiring decisions. Emotional stress has a way of clouding thinking!

How to Treat a Friend
in The Interview

BRAD PEDERSEN

B rad is an entrepreneur and investor that has built several consumer product companies that have collectively shipped billions of products worldwide. Brad co-founded Pela; a direct to consumer brand that is creating a waste free future by designing and manufacturing environmentally sensible consumer products.

Brad's worst hire took place at a time when his company was evolving and growing, and there was a distinct need for a vice president to work closely with the team and client base. Due to the specialization of the company and industry requirements, Brad needed to hire someone who knew both the clients and the marketplace as there was no time for training or waiting for the new vice president to get up to speed in the industry.

Brad had a long-time friend who was in the industry and he thought he knew this friend well enough to consider them as a candidate for the role. Having someone join the company that would be both a friend and business associate was something Brad thought would be a win/win situation. As an added bonus, the candidate had a successful business track record and great sales demeanor. Due to the already established personal relationship, the company decided to bypass the interview process and moved quickly into an employment agreement that provided the candidate too much freedom and autonomy in the role.

Brad very quickly realized the juxtaposition of having a friend, and then requiring that friend to report to you in a business situation. It very quickly altered the relationship. The new hire turned out to be a resounding success in the sales department, but their negative attitude with the team offset the positive sales to the point that Brad had to let the new hire go. This bad hire not only caused the loss of a friendship but also the loss of valuable clients that were taken when the candidate joined a competing firm.

COST:

Significant and irreparable—this worst hire was one of many reasons the company closed.

BRAD PEDERSEN

Brad is the Co-Founder and acting Chairman of Open Mind Developments corporation. The company owns the Pela brand and is committed to creating a waste free future by making consumer products out of biodegradable and environmentally sensible materials. Brad's experience with developing products comes from a long history in the toy industry where Brad most recently was the Co-Founder of Basic Fun.

Be extremely careful when you consider hiring a friend. If they will be reporting to you, expect the relationship to change. During the interview process, treat a friend like any other candidate. Be aware that the boss-employee relationship will affect the friendship.

Falling in Love with Your Candidate

PAUL SHEKOSKI

aul Shekoski is President and CEO of Primex Inc. He has been in high technology, business development, sales and marketing, and engineering roles throughout his career. Paul is involved in most hires within his company.

Paul's company required some new thinking and leadership within their growing sales team. The company was expanding, new technology was being deployed to new and existing customers, the markets were constantly changing and the sales team needed to adapt. There was a growing need for the team to learn to sell to different stake holders within their market, and this would require a new leader in the sales department to lead this change. Paul and his management team made a decision to look outside the company for this leader hoping to hire a candidate who would bring new thinking and perspective to meet the growth challenges of their business.

A search firm was hired and before long, a short list was presented to the team. After initial interviews, one candidate stood out from the rest. As Paul said, "We fell in love with the candidate, and we let our guard down." What is interesting regarding this worst hire is that the assessment tools used indicated concerns, specifically in regard to the way this candidate might treat subordinates. The team read the assessment report, skimmed over the red flags, then tucked it away in a file and proceeded to conduct very superficial references which all checked out.

Once the candidate was hired, Paul started to hear grumblings from the sales team, specifically related to the way they were being spoken to and managed. It wasn't long before Paul heard that the team was ready to abandon the company. Paul stepped in, and the sales leader was let go within a year of the hire.

COST:

Over $350,000.

PAUL SHEKOSKI

Paul is the Chief Executive Officer and a member of the Board of Directors at the Primex Family of Companies, which help people stay connected to their world via IOT sensors in time, temperature and weather instrument to retail, commercial and consumer markets. Paul joined the 75-year-old privately held company in 2005 as the first outside CEO to accelerate the Primex Family of Companies growth in partnership with the Founder.

Hiring is an emotional event for everyone involved. It is easy to fall in love with a candidate in an interview. If you pay for a service to assess the candidate and information is provided concerning the candidate's background, don't ignore the information it gives you—use it.

Your Hire Is an Extension of Yourself

ALBERT ATKINS

Albert fast tracked his career into senior management at a young age while working on three continents, driving change in different cultures. Identifying and developing talent is a passion of Alberts and has been his cornerstone for building strong, profitable teams.

When Albert arrived at one of his cross country moves in the role of general manager, he quickly recognized that his inherited sales management team had too much similarity in their look, gender, thinking and approach to business. Albert's #1 objective was to hire a new sales manager that would break the mould of the existing team and be a spark for change. Albert initiated a search and landed an outstanding candidate, and the hire was made. Looking back, Albert believes there was too much focus on this new hire being the much-needed spark, and not enough time on the onboarding process that would integrate them and allow them to act as a change agent within the team. Albert can point to this lack of structured onboarding that set the stage for his worst hiring mistake.

Albert can distinctly remember the shocked look in the executive management's eyes when the new hire presented their enthusiastic, but unrealistic sales plan to upper management. Management had very specific requirements for these meetings and one of them was "realistic sales targets" with 100% conviction of achieving the numbers. Anything under 100% was unacceptable! When the candidate was asked where they believed the territory would end up at the end of the year, the answer was an enthusiastic "I can guarantee we will achieve 90%." The damage was done, and the new hire had no idea of the landmine they had just stepped into. This embarrassing moment could have been avoided through proper onboarding and understanding what management expected in these types of meetings.

COST:

The biggest cost was Albert's credibility with both his sales team and the executive leadership team.

ALBERT ATKINS

Albert is a senior executive with a leading multinational Industrial Gas company. He has lived and worked in 4 different countries, on 3 different continents, with experience ranging from operations to HR to strategic planning. He has a proven track record of leading across cultures, driving change, delivering results, and developing top talent. Albert holds a degree in Mechanical Engineering from Texas A&M University and Executive Leadership certificates from both the Rotman School of Management at the University of Toronto and the London Business School.

Protect your hard-earned credibility! You put your own reputation on the line when hiring someone into the company. The new hire becomes an extension of your management and assessment abilities, and any positive or negatives that arise from the hire will be ultimately tied back to you!

No Pat Answers, Thank you

BRIAN SEMKIW

Brian is a seasoned business leader who has started companies and successfully taken them public. He is a determined leader with the single-minded discipline of a professional engineer.

Brian and a team of investors were involved in a start-up when he experienced his worst hire. The company had little revenue at the time, but lots of expenses and they needed to hire some top talent quickly. One of the immediate needs included someone to develop and implement contracts and corporate governance required by the newly formed board. Brian was introduced to a past acquaintance who was looking for work and had the skills required for corporate governance work. Due to the financial situation of the start-up and the potential upside growth of the company, Brian was able to negotiate a starting salary below market pay at the time. That, coupled with the fact that the candidate was an acquaintance, cleared the way for the company to forge ahead and make an offer forgoing any due diligence, interview, or references. The offer was made and quickly accepted.

Before long, all hell broke loose, and the board was

NO PAT ANSWERS, THANK YOU

thrown into turmoil due in large part to the new employee's divisive action. Within months of the hire, Brian's new company and board were in real danger of losing control. It took much effort and significant time to finally rid themselves of the employee but not before incurring immense cost to the company. Brian later discovered that this bad hire had created the same turmoil in some of their past roles with the same negative results.

COST:

Over $2,000,000 and setting the company back a full year.

BRIAN SEMKIW

Brian, Founder and CEO, is responsible for the strategic vision of KarbonKleen. Prior to founding KarbonKleen, Mr. Semkiw has experienced a long track record of success from leading Carta Worldwide to becoming a global FinTech leader and co-founding Rand Engineering, Engineering.com and Rand Worldwide. Profit Magazine recognized Rand as one of Canada's fastest growth companies and Brian was awarded Entrepreneur of the Year in 1996. Brian's formal education includes a BSc. from the University of Toronto.

Never bypass a proven hiring process, even if you know the person. Talk to legitimate references and do not take pat answers. Ask tough questions that require the reference to either disclose the truth or indicate by their hesitation that there might be some warning signs. You will never discover disruptive behavior in an interview.

Promoting Your Top Salesperson to Manager

TIM CERNY

T im was previously EVP of a large staffing firm and his clients were the Who's Who of North America's business community. In his 8 years in the role, Tim hired over 100 employees in different roles.

Tim's company was known for hiring new graduates and grooming them into different roles within the company. Tim's worst hire story is based around an internal move of a superstar sales professional who had aspirations of being a sales manager. This particular salesperson was well known within the company due to their high performance as an individual contributor. Like many good salespeople, this employee loved the thrill of the hunt but was not very good at the operational details of the job. Their attributes were geared towards being more of a lone wolf than a team player.

Ultimately, an internal posting for a sales manager role was placed, and the application was open to anyone. Many in the department were concerned when they heard the superstar salesperson had applied for the role. Tim was completely on board with the idea of this candidate applying for the role as he truly felt he would be able to mold the employee into a successful sales manager. The promotion took place and after only 3 months in the new role, complaints began to trickle in from internal team members saying that the new sales manager was keenly interested in their own sales production but not quite as willing to work with the team. Within 6 months, Tim had to step in and demote the candidate back to his previous role. After a month, the salesperson left for a competitor and over time was successful at taking key accounts to their new employer.

COST:

Over $1,000,000.

TIM CERNY

Tim Cerny is the CEO at Safety Net, an IT Managed Service Provider in Traverse City, MI. Prior positions include President of American Healthcare Services Association and EVP of TEKsystems Canada. Tim earned his bachelor's degree in Business Administration and Communications at Hope College and currently serves as President of the Traverse City Junior Golf Board of Directors.

The attributes you see in an employee or candidate are hardwired, and coaching and guidance will have little change or impact on the person's actions in the long run. Be aware that most top sales performers do not make great managers, and you should be extremely careful before promoting one into a management role.

Take Reference Comments Down a Notch

PEDER ENHORNING

eder has spent most of his career in the world of technology in the capacity of sales, sales management, and CEO of his own analytics company. His worst hire took place when he was a sales manager in a small software company with twenty employees and only a few sales professionals. It was imperative that Peder's hire would meet and exceed their expected sales goals. He was looking to hire a star sales rep and turned to a recruiting firm to assist in the search.

The challenge with this hire was that what seemed to be a positive was disguised and eventually turned out to be the problem. The candidate was assertive and aggressive. Not confrontational, but a very tough negotiator for his salary, commission, and sales territory. He was hired with the assumption he would be very hard-working and a good negotiator, dedicated to get the best deal for the company. Instead, he only cared about himself.

It was the reference checks that should have stopped

the hire from taking place. Peder's assertion is that most references lie, or at very least, exaggerate. After all, they have been hand-picked by the candidate. If a reference says the candidate is "outstanding," it probably means they are "good," and if they say they are "good", they are not worth hiring. When Peder asked the references to describe the candidate in different elements of the role, he received descriptions like "good," "okay," and "alright". In retrospect, those were red flags.

The result of this hire turned out to be a sales rep who was extremely demanding on resources, always looking to other team members to do the hard work for them, focusing solely on their personal goals and agenda. Once when blaming his failure on the company not providing enough quality leads, the conversation escalated to a shouting match. His presence on the team created a great deal of anguish for Peder and the other employees in the company.

COST:

Lost business opportunities, compensation, and staff morale put the cost in the $600,000 range.

PEDER ENHORNING

Peder is CEO of Unilytics Corp., which provides business intelligence and data analytics consulting services to a broad range of clients. Prior to starting Unilytics in 2001, Peder founded a medical manufacturing firm and earlier in his career held various sales and sales management roles in the computer software industry.

References typically embellish the quality and character of a candidate for many reasons. Take the comments from a reference down one notch from what you are told. If the reference describes the candidate as "excellent", they really mean "very good," "very good" means "good," and "good" means "less than average." Be careful if you receive too many "goods."

Can Your Candidate Take Criticism?

ROBIN SMITH

Robin is a perfect example of a CEO and business owner who is an expert in his field but challenged in getting the hiring right when it comes to key technical staff. His OMNI channel integration firm is always in need of top-quality technical talent to meet the ever-changing landscape of their global clients.

Like most CEOs, Robin can look back with regret on difficult technical hiring challenges he has faced over the years. His worst hiring mistake was two-fold, as he and his team got this hire wrong twice in a row. Once is painful, but twice is incrementally more expensive and had a significant impact on business growth. The role was a mobile application developer, and the person who was hired as a replacement for the initial bad hire lasted only three months, quitting during their probationary period.

The first twelve months went smoothly enough. Robin and his team never had to confront, challenge, or critique this software developer during the infancy stage of the mobile application project. However, once team meetings reviewed and discussed in greater detail and depth the work of the developer, offering potential new ideas and constructive criticisms, things went rapidly downhill. A buried nerve within the candidate's make-up was struck, only revealed during heated team discussions. As Robin reflected on this hiring mistake, he realized that the references that had been conducted in the hiring stage had been centered around technical skills with no concern for the temperament of the candidate when challenged or criticized. They were a time bomb ready and waiting to explode, and the impact was felt throughout the office. Robin had to act and remove the employee after one of his staff was directly threatened. As Robin commented, "They simply had a tough time with an authority challenging their work and ideas."

COST:

Over a year's worth of software development due to the majority of the development work having to be rewritten. Estimated cost $500,000 to $750,000.

ROBIN SMITH

Robin is the CEO and Co-Founder of Virtual Logistics Inc. a data integration company. Prior to starting VL, Robin worked in East Africa and the Middle East as Director of Business Development for a major Telecommunication company. Robin earned his BA from the University of Toronto and an MA with Webster University in Vienna, Austria.

There are hidden issues that candidates cover up in the interview. Be prepared to add situational interview questions in your assessment of candidates to attempt to uncover flawed character traits. When talking to references, ask questions that include the candidate's ability to take criticism and deal with authority.

Don't Call My Boss for a Reference

CRAIG BISSETT

Over the past 30 plus years of being in the HR marketplace, I have seen and experienced many poor hiring decisions. At the time of my worst hire, our clients were dealing with a high demand for specific technology expertise that was not available in North America. We were approached to assist in recruiting and relocating approximately 100 highly skilled programmers and related professionals from around the world and move them to North America. But first we needed to hire an inhouse immigration lawyer who would travel to these locations worldwide to expedite the required immigration papers for each successful candidate.

We posted our requirements online and in a short period of time received a number of resumes that caught our attention as the candidates had been part of large and very reputable legal firms specializing in immigration. An offer was presented to a candidate who had impressed our team in the interview. All that was needed was to complete a few references from the candidate's current employer. In a very convincing presentation, the candidate sold us a story as to why we could not call their most recent boss. We accepted this well-planned story, conducted one reference from an employer who had worked with the candidate 10 years prior, and made an offer.

The new lawyer immediately began extensive travel and although the need to be budget conscious had been very explicit, numerous flights were booked business class and there was always a "story" behind the reasoning for that. Furthermore, incomplete, late and error filled files were causing our clients costly delays. We quickly moved to let our lawyer go, and were served notice for wrongful dismissal. We later discovered this person had been put on probation at their last job and was about to be fired when we hired them.

COST:

Hard cost of over $80,000 and loss of clients worth $500,000 in revenue.

CRAIG BISSETT

Craig is President of Hire Results Ltd, a Human Capital assessment firm established in 2002. He is the creator and developer of the Hiring Simulation Assessment process which allows hiring teams to Test Drive candidates before making a hiring decision. He has held Partnership and General Management roles in some of Canada's leading Human Capital firms. Craig is a graduate of Ryerson University.

Don't allow a candidate to smooth talk their way out of providing you and your team the key information you require to make a smart and logical hiring decision. If you require additional information from a candidate, make this information part of the requirement before making an offer. There is always a reason why someone does not want to provide information—dig deep and understand why.

Afterword

At the start of our book, you read about the wise prospector who understood how to sift a panful of rocks and mud down to a few valuable nuggets. Our hope is that you have received some valuable lessons from our contributors and have tucked away a few nuggets for use when hiring tomorrow or a few years down the road.

The My Worst Hire & What I Learned From It book is intended to be a resource for you to read and then refer back to the valuable nuggets time and time again before you embark on your next hiring project. If you are part of a team, we encourage you to order the book in quantities of 10 or more and receive a 20% discount on each book. Our goal is to have this book on every hiring manager's desk (Intern to Executive) to allow organizations to reap the rewards of quality, productive hires.

Drop us a note at comments@craigbissett.com and let us know how you have implemented one or more of these learning nuggets. Feel free to send our website and book link to your friends and business associates at www.myworsthire. com

Keep an eye out for our second book in our "My Worst Series" titled, My Worst Interview & What I Learned From It (from the candidate's perspective). If you have a story and you would like to be a contributor to our next book, email us at contributors@craigbissett.com.

Wishing you successful hiring!

About the Author

Craig Bissett is the founder of Hire Results Ltd and creator of the Hiring Simulation Assessment® process. His company and proprietary Simulation process have been implemented in thousands of hiring situations over the years throughout North America.

If you would like to book Craig to speak with your hiring teams or provide a keynote talk, you can connect with his team at contact@craigbissett.com.